OTTAWA
REWIND

A BOOK OF CURIOS
AND MYSTERIES

OTTAWA
REWIND

A BOOK OF CURIOS
AND MYSTERIES

ANDREW KING

OTTAWA
PRESS AND
PUBLISHING

ottawapressandpublishing.com

Copyright © Andrew King 2019

ISBN (pbk.) 978-1-988437-34-7
ISBN (EPUB) 978-1-988437-35-4
ISBN (MOBI) 978-1-988437-36-1

Printed and bound in Canada

Design and composition: Magdalene Carson at New Leaf Publication Design

For my parents, Carol and Dave,
who instilled in me a sense of adventure and
a love of history "in our own backyard."

Also, to the many readers of Ottawa Rewind
who always encouraged me to one day write a book.

TABLE OF CONTENTS

INTRODUCTION

Since the dawn of time the Ottawa area has been a source of intriguing geography, history and more than its fair share of mystery. The history of our region goes back 13,000 years to when the Ottawa Valley was a vast, creature-filled ocean called the Champlain Sea. We cannot begin to imagine the mysteries that would have been found in that once great ocean.

When the Champlain Sea retreated, the confluence of three major rivers made Ottawa an important trade and travel area for thousands of years. The people who first travelled and settled in the region made it a site for camps and battles and a centre for trade, involving people from across North America, that sprung up around the Chaudiere Falls. Early European explorers — including perhaps the greatest of them all, Samuel de Champlain — made their way through the Ottawa region and marveled at how beautiful and special it was.

When the first European settlers arrived in 1800 (they were actually Americans) the area slowly began its journey through time to become a focal point for the lumber industry, with streets and roads emerging from overgrown wilderness and swamps.

Soon after, Ottawa — or Bytown, as it was then called — was recognized for its geographic and strategic importance, and the Rideau Canal was constructed. All this history was years before the game-changing event that came to define our city — Queen Victoria, in 1857, choosing Ottawa to become the capital of Canada.

Government and mysteries seem to go hand in hand, as you'll soon see in this book, and Queen Victoria's decision put Ottawa on the world stage with its architectural riddles, top-tier secrets, and political tales.

It is these facets of Ottawa's history that have always intrigued me — its transformation from a backwoods settlement to a strategic and political capital, with all the amazing stuff that happened in-between. Our city unfairly got the moniker "the city that fun forgot" because of its bureaucracy and smaller size, but we have history that other cities can only wish they possessed.

In this book I have collected my favourite historical tales and places, many long forgotten, or even lost to time. Using modern research tools, on-the-ground exploration and old-fashioned detective work, I have been able to track down Ottawa's first pub, a lost Iroquois village near Prescott, and a steamship at the bottom of Britannia Bay that once carried the King of England.

But history is not only what you read in schoolbooks. Not only tales about the King of England. You need more than that for a full rendering of any city. In a political city such as Ottawa, this is sometimes difficult to achieve — getting people to remember that there is a city beneath Parliament Hill.

So in *Ottawa Rewind* I have investigated other historical mysteries from the nation's capital, riddles that came to me one day and soon needed to be investigated. Whatever happened to Ottawa's first Tiki bar? Was there really a Playboy Club in Vanier? And what's with all those pyramids at the old city hall?

I hope you will enjoy reading about these mysteries, and curios, as much as I have enjoyed discovering and writing about them. I encourage you to share this information with others, and who knows, maybe there's another book yet to be written, about things that have yet to be discovered about our city.

Andrew King
2019

ACKNOWLEDGMENTS

Ottawa Rewind has been a rewarding and entertaining side project for me since I began posting stories back in 2013. As I have conducted my research and gone on my explorations, I have had the help of a great many people, none more important than the readers and fans of *Ottawa Rewind* who have encouraged me to continue publishing these stories.

The stories and research material I have been sifting through were all made possible by numerous institutions and companies that make this information available to the public. It truly is a wonderful age to be a researcher, and I would like to thank the Ottawa Public Library, Library and Archives Canada, the City Of Ottawa, Google News Archives, Google Maps and GeoOttawa.

In a world of digital resources at your fingertips, it is easy to forget about good old-fashioned libraries and books, but printed books have provided me with many pieces of valuable information that were never found online. Never underestimate the power of a real book or a real map and many thanks go out to anyone who works at a library or bookstore.

I'd like to thank my friend Glen Gower, of *OttawaStart,* for providing a platform to share my stories with the public. Glen shares my passion for local history and would often join me on my adventures and explorations. I'd also like to thank Keith Bonnell, former deputy editor at the *Ottawa Citizen,* who gave me the chance to write a regular column for the *Citizen.* Not only did Keith give me a wider audience for my local history adventures, he actually paid me.

It is with that same appreciation I'd like to thank Ron Corbett of Ottawa Press and Publishing. Ron's passion for regional publishing, and his support of the *Ottawa Rewind* project, made this book possible. Designer Magdalene Carson of New Leaf Publication Design did an amazing job compiling and formatting my stories into a beautifully presented book.

Last, but never least, I'd like to thank my parents for instilling in me a sense of adventure: sailing around Lake Ontario, taking me to museums, and joining me on many of these adventures. The same goes for my dear Ali, who has put up with countless mosquito bites trudging to remote locations, with only the occasional eye roll.

It has been a distinct pleasure creating this material over the years, and I want to thank you, the reader, for holding this book in your hands right now.

OTTAWA
REWIND

A BOOK OF CURIOS
AND MYSTERIES

THE STRANGE DISAPPEARANCE OF THE *ANN SISSON*

In 1860 the Prince of Wales, the future king of England, travelled up the Ottawa River aboard the steamship *"Ann Sisson."* The ship was lost beneath the waves in 1871. This is the story of the search to find it.

A Royal Visit

The year was 1860 and Queen Victoria had recently selected Ottawa to be the permanent capital of the new Province of Canada. Yet the Queen would never visit Canada. It was said she despised traveling on water due to seasickness. Instead, she sent her son Albert Edward, Prince of Wales (later King Edward VII), in her place to make the first official royal visit to the Province of Canada.

The eighteen-year-old prince would visit Newfoundland, the Maritimes and Canada (later Ontario and Quebec.) While here he would open the Victoria Bridge between the Island of Montreal and the south shore of the St Lawrence River. And under full masonic ceremony, the future Grand Master of the Freemasons United Grand Lodge of England would also lay the cornerstone for our future Parliament Buildings.

After a whirlwind tour of Ottawa meeting residents and business leaders, the future king would board the 139-foot, side-wheeler steamship *Ann Sisson* for a tour up the Ottawa River. The steamship

The Prince of Wales laying the cornerstone for our future Parliament Buildings, 1860.

was outfitted for the royal journey; its usual lumber ship duties suspended and passenger accommodations added. Owned by Brewster & Mulholland from Montreal, the company outfitted the ship for the prince and his entourage to venture north on the river.

The prince left Aylmer and steamed away in the royally appointed ship and as evening approached, he decided to stay overnight in Quyon, Quebec. The next day, the *Ann Sisson* docked in Pontiac where the prince boarded a horse railway that took him on the remainder of his Ottawa Valley tour. The royal steamship then returned to its duties as a lumber steamer. It became a passenger steamer in 1863, transporting passengers between Aylmer/Ottawa and Pontiac under the Union Forwarding and Railway Company. Records show that in 1871 the once regal ship was stripped, burned and abandoned in the Ottawa River.

So where is the Royal Wreck? I became intrigued with finding this important piece of Ottawa history and began a quest to find the *Ann Sisson*.

The Demise of the *Ann Sisson*

A quick Google search revealed I was not the only one interested in finding the ship. Britannia resident Mike Kaulbars has written extensively about her on his blog *Britannia: A History*. His research deduced that the ship was abandoned somewhere in the area of Britannia Bay.

↻ The *Ann Sisson* as it appeared at the transfer dock in Pontiac, Quebec.

The *Ann Sisson* had been built in Aylmer and took passengers and lumber back and forth between Pontiac and Aylmer. According to the book *A Foregone Fleet: A Pictorial History Of Steam-Driven Paddleboats on the Ottawa River* by Andrew E. Lamarinde and Gilles L. Seguin, the Ann Sisson was built in 1857. The ship had a wooden hull braced internally with a series of built-up longitudinal timbers, and the massive iron steam engine weighed 108 metric tons. The keel of the ship had to be strengthened to prevent the engine from breaking through the bottom of the hull. Iron fasteners would hold wooden planks running longitudinally.

When the Prince of Wales arrived in Ottawa for his grand tour of North America, the *Ann Sisson* was only three years old, so it would have been a fairly robust new ship. Preparations were made for the royal entourage, including cabin appointments for the four-hour journey to Quyon, where the royal party made a surprise stay at the only inn in the village, with plates and cutlery being borrowed from residents to accommodate the unscheduled visit.

After the departure of the prince the next day, the *Ann Sisson* went back to hauling timber along the river until, in 1863, it became a full-time passenger steamer captained by Denis Murphy. Murphy would later form a partnership in the D. Murphy and Company, which mainly transported lumber and coal on the Ottawa River and Rideau Canal. (In 1902 Murphy would represent the riding of Ottawa in the Legislative Assembly of Ontario as a Conservative member.)

Having fulfilled its duties on the Ottawa River, records show that the *Ann Sisson* was then unceremoniously stripped of all its valuable

Steamship travel up the Ottawa River aboard one of the 19th-century steamships.

hardware and components, and burned, left to sink some-where in the very waters that once carried the future king of England.

The Search

Mike Kaulbars and his research on the *Ann Sisson* led me to *The Carleton Saga*, a book by Harry and Olive Walker, where it was stated that a lighthouse keeper at Britannia by the name of Robert Winthrop navigated in a boat around what he said was the wreck of a "famous boat of the Ottawa Valley fleet, the *Ann Sissons*."

The ship was apparently beached and burned near the lighthouse. Kaulbars also uncovered information that a wreck was found in Britannia waters during the summer of 1962, but it was misidentified as the steamship *Albert*, which was almost identical to the *Ann Sisson* in both construction and size. Yet that ship, the *Albert*, was recorded as being dissembled in Quyon in 1917. No further information on this mysterious shipwreck could be found.

Honing In

One of the greatest resources I have for my historical research is the amazing "geoOttawa" map program provided online by the City Of Ottawa. Using aerial photographs from 1928 onwards, it can give an accurate representation of what the city looked like from the air over the years. Using this, I was able to find the earliest aerial photo for the Britannia region, which happened to be 1958. Scanning this old aerial photograph, I noticed a curious looking shape under the waves. Zooming in on the shadowy shape offshore, it looked remarkably like the outline of a ship.

Using the scale of the map, the mystery shape measured out to 140 feet in length, an almost exact match to the length of the *Ann Sisson*. Overlaying that 1958 position with a current 2018 aerial map, though, did not show any signs of what might have been our shipwreck.

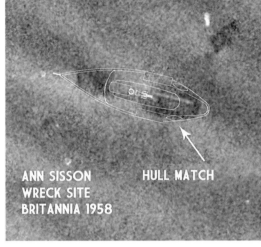

From a 1958 aerial photo of Britannia Bay.

Locking in the GPS coordinates of where the wreck was supposed to be, I downloaded an app on my cell phone that tracks the user's GPS position and displays the coordinates, so you can walk around to your desired position.

A good app. Except that my location was under water. I was going to need some help.

Archeologists Join In

I reached out to Ben Mortimer and Nadine Kopp, archeologists with the Paterson Group, an archeological consulting service in the Ottawa area. Kopp's specialty is "underwater archeology," so her knowledge about 19th century ships and marine construction would provide a welcome set of skills to hopefully identify any remains we might find.

With our search team assembled, we headed out to the old cottage village of Belltown that straddles Britannia Bay and headed to the shoreline. Knowing we'd be searching underwater, we brought the appropriate equipment to try to locate the wreck and possibly record its remains.

What would be left, if anything? This ship was from the era of the American Civil War, and wrecks from that era are still being found intact, so I kept positive that something would be visible. Wading deeper and deeper into the river and farther from shore with cell phone GPS coordinates flashing before me, something caught my eye in the dark and murky waters: a sand-covered square timber.

With much of the bottom of the Ottawa River being strewn with old lumber from its days as a conduit for timber rafts, I thought it was probably just an old log. Yet following the squared timber it led to other squared timbers, iron fasteners, hull planking, and the tell tale pieces of a ship.

Kopp quickly examined the wooden planks and hull pieces strewn about and assessed that these were indeed the remains of a ship. Further study showed the remains were that of a mid-1800s ship, evidence being in the construction techniques visible in the wreck.

Lying underwater, out of view for decades, the ship's charred wood revealed its fate — it had been burned and left to sink into the sand.

The Last Voyage

Kopp explained that without definitive proof it was not possible to confirm that what we found that day was the *Ann Sisson*. Cross-referencing the construction of the wreck with blueprints would verify it, but those blueprints may be impossible to find.

What we are left with is a shipwreck of mid-1800s design and construction, lying at the bottom of Britannia Bay, where it was reported the *Ann Sisson* was laid to rest. It seems at least plausible, if not probable, that a very important piece of Ottawa history has remained underwater for 150 years. I would love to see the remnants of this 19th-century steamship be recovered and put in a museum.

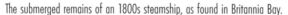

The submerged remains of an 1800s steamship, as found in Britannia Bay.

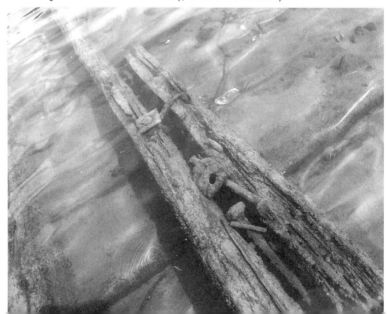

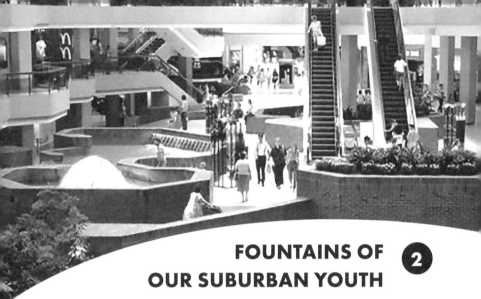

FOUNTAINS OF OUR SUBURBAN YOUTH

Searching for the Last Shopping-Mall Water Fountain

"Meetcha at the fountain"

That was a phrase many teenagers of the '80s used when they wanted to meet up with friends at the local mall. Before Snapchat or texting, '80s kids had to phone each other, often from kitchen phones with parents listening, and saying "the fountain"— was an understood term of reference. Every shopping mall had a water fountain

It was a different era, and the shopping malls of the '80s were extravagant retail meccas, a place for us awkward kids to spend our allowance on a bag of Kernels, some posters from Discus, video games from CompuCentre, all done under the dappled rays of a sky-lit roof.

Appointed with soothing beige tile work, usually complemented with a mix of wood and teal-dusty-rose trim, there was nothing quite like the malls of the '80s. In addition to their era-specific decor splendor, they almost always had another common feature: a massive water fountain.

Spraying a geyser of chlorinated water into the dry mall air, its burbling sounds and circular construction were always a welcome and soothing sight to behold, a place to relax, congregate and meet up with your school pals for an afternoon of hanging out at the mall. Yet this once core landmark has now vanished from most shopping malls, their demise brought on by the downward spiral of the mall retail model.

Before they disappear completely, let's tease our hair, pull up our tube socks and take a take a step back in time for a look at Ottawa's fountains of our youth.

Mall Mania

The shopping mall was a post-war retail concept primarily based on the transition of residential areas to outside the downtown core. Servicing these new suburbs with shopping "centres" involved an enclosed space with stores that were indoor, accessible only by car. Ottawa has its share of early-50s malls, but the focus of this piece is on malls that featured opulent water fountains.

An American shopping centre developer by the name of Alfred Taubman revolutionized shopping malls by introducing tiled floors instead of carpet, indoor fountains, and two levels, allowing a shopper to make a circuit of all the stores. Daylight was filtered through glass skylights making it seem like the afternoon was lasting longer, which encouraged shoppers to linger the whole day.

The water fountain and accompanying greenery of the new malls was intended to create an "oasis" for the shopper, a place to relax and enjoy the shopping experience, like going on a vacation. Under the calming sounds of burbling water amidst lush tropical plants, you

The shopping malls of the '70s and '80s were designed to be an oasis, even for smokers.

ALMUTH LUTKENHAUS

born in Germany. Came to Canada in 1966.
1948-1952 studied at the Art Colleges (Werkkunst-
schulen) at Dortmund and Münster,
Germany.
1952-1966 permanent lecturer at the Community
College (Volkshochschule) of Hamm,
Germany.
Won by competition approximately 20
commissions for major bronze sculptures and sculptural walls in public buildings in Germany.
Since 1968 teaching at Mohawk College, Hamilton,
Ontario and other institutions.
Major commissions: Civic Centre (1967)
and St. James Church, Oakville. Fountain sculptures (12′ high) for Belleville,
Ontario, and Trois Rivières, Québec. In
1972 fountain sculptures (15′ high) for
Bayshore Shopping Centre, Ottawa.
Monumental relief for City Hall, Toronto.
1973 Won two competitions for double sculp-

The iconic bronze sculpture at Bayshore was created by German artist, Almuth Lütkenhaus. Studying her craft in Germany until she moved to Canada in 1966, Lütkenhaus was commissioned to do the fifteen-foot-high bronze sculpture in 1972.

could buy your slacks. The fountain was where parents would tell kids to meet if they got separated, a rendezvous place, and a spot for kids to toss coins into the depths of the crystal clear waters in hopes that a special wish would come true.

One of the most notable mall fountains in Ottawa was the one at Bayshore Shopping Centre. Opened in 1973, Bayshore featured an epic central fountain with a commissioned sculpture of "very thin people" dancing in the spray. Most of Ottawa that shopped there between 1973 and the late-'80s remember this very memorable fountain, until it mysteriously disappeared during renovations.

A common misconception about that fountain sculpture is that it was moved to Sparks Street. A similar looking sculpture does exist on Sparks Street, but that one was commissioned by E.R. Fisher when the men's store was down there. That sculpture is called *Joy* by the late Bruce Garner. The Bayshore sculpture was made by German artist, Almuth Lütkenhaus.

Prominently installed amidst a geyser of water in the centre of the mall, Lütkenhaus's sculpture was later removed when the mall underwent renovations. Where it went to is the subject of ongoing conjecture in the city, although one possibility has always been Michael Cowpland's backyard.

One possibile location for the missing Bayshore sculpture has always been Michael Cowpland's backyard.

Hazeldean Mall is the last Ottawa shopping mall to still operate a water fountain.

Fading Fountains

Place d'Orleans Mall expanded to its current size in 1990 and had a grand reopening. It would be one of the last enclosed malls built in Canada. Its massive fountain, once an illuminated Vegas-style light show, has since been removed, the area now used to display automobiles and other retail products.

Along with the water features, the tropical plants that used to provide a foliaged refuge for shoppers during the bitter winter months have also been removed from most shopping centres, replaced with a clean, sterile aesthetic that resembles Apple's minimalist environment.

Hazeldean Mall, which opened on October 30, 1979, is the last of Ottawa's shopping malls to still operate a water fountain. A trickling stepped fountain that once ran from one end of the mall to the other has now been reduced in size, but still functions.

The once bustling meccas of our youth, the prime Saturday hangout where we'd hit the Orange Julius, Discus, Zellers, and the arcade, are now distant memories for Gen Xers. If I had known, I would have tossed a dime into their bubbling waters, wishing they would never disappear.

READER' REMARKS

Great story! I seem to recall Bayshore having two fountains, the large one, which truly was an oasis, and a much smaller one, which also had a more modest sculpture by the same artist. That smaller one was what I thought ended up on Sparks Street. — *Ward*

Your story brought back some good memories! I worked at the Bay at the Bayshore Mall from 1973 to 1978. It was interesting to find out where the fountain statue ended up. I love your sleuthing skills. — *Catherine*

I believe cost and making malls more profitable has a lot to do with getting rid of fountains and greenery. Same thing happened in office buildings in Ottawa. It simply cost too much in maintenance, so they disappeared in an age of efficiency. — *Larry*

Good job on the research! This was interesting. — *Jen*

Thank you for finding this out. I always wondered what happened to that sculpture and knew it wasn't the one on Sparks Street. I hung out at the Bayshore Mall in my high school years in the early 1980s and that fountain was a landmark. — *Richard*

Isn't it funny how, sometimes things disappear so gradually, you never even notice they're gone. Thanks for noticing, Andrew. That Bayshore fountain was certainly a highpoint of the mall. I don't know if it's the absence of fountains and greenery that make me shun malls today, but you're right that they look sterile and antiseptic. — *Dwight*

OTTAWA'S SECRET SOLSTICE PYRAMIDS

③

The winter solstice is an astronomical event usually occurring around December 21 that signifies the shortest day and longest night of the year. Since ancient times the solstice has been considered a significant event, one that has guided cultures and led to celebrations and ceremonies around such archeological sites as Stonehenge in England and Newgrange in Ireland. These sites, along with pyramids in Egypt and Mexico, appear to have been carefully aligned with the winter solstice sunrise and the winter solstice sunset.

It seems unusual that we would find any modern monuments designed to celebrate this ancient tradition, but whether by coincidence or deliberate planning, Ottawa seems to have its very own secret solstice pyramids.

The Safdie Mystery

Green Island is just east of Ottawa's downtown core, a significant island on the Rideau River right before it converges with the Ottawa River in a dramatic dual waterfall. Once a sacred site for Indigenous peoples, Green Island became the site of Ottawa City Hall in 1958. In 1988 it was redesigned in a bold new plan by architect Moshe Safdie. Safdie's redesign of the original 1958 City Hall included a number of carefully positioned pyramids throughout the island, four to be exact, in various shapes and sizes.

I have always been perplexed by these unusual glass pyramids, as they seem to have little function other than to be aesthetically incorporated into Safdie's reimagined city hall. Safdie may be best known for his architecture in Montreal known as Habitat 67, which pioneered the design and implementation of three-dimensional, pre-fabricated units. It was a central feature of Expo 67 and an important development in architectural history.

In 1988 Ottawa mayor Jim Durrell wanted to expand City Hall on Green Island and architect Moshe Safdie was selected for the redesign. Soon Safdie and the city were at odds as Safdie demanded a higher fee and wanted some unique features incorporated into the new design. The redesign cost 72 million dollars and was much larger than the city needed with much of the space sitting vacant for years.

So why *are* there four pyramids incorporated into this design? Well, one possible explanation — each pyramid is aligned with the position of the sun during the winter solstice.

Solstice Pyramids

Using an app called Sun Surveyor to superimpose the position of the sunrise and sunset of the winter solstice reveals that Safdie's pyramids are in perfect alignment with both the solstice sunrise and sunset. Whether this is by pure coincidence or was carefully planned is unknown, but the application clearly illustrates these solstice alignments.

Pyramid 1 is a large pyramid on the south end of the complex, cut in half with a truncated cone. Placing the centre position on the winter solstice, the sun sets on exactly the westerly edge of the pyramid and there is even a landscape feature marking the sunset position.

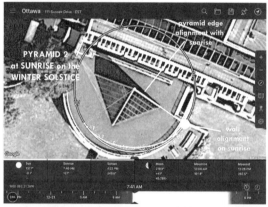

Pyramid 2 is a smaller half-pyramid on the west side of the complex and the centre position aligns with the sunrise of the winter solstice. This half-pyramid's alignment with the sunrise on the winter solstice seems too perfect to be coincidental.

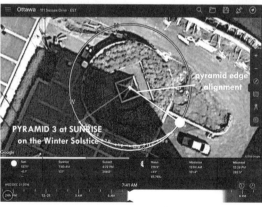

Pyramid 3 is a smaller pyramid on the north-east corner of the complex and it is a full pyramid whose south edge corner is also in alignment with the sunrise of the winter solstice.

Did Safdie intentionally position these glass pyramids to align with the winter solstice? Alas, I do not have his phone number. But you can see if for yourself, on the next winter solstice, by taking a stroll to the Green Island Pyramids.

THE PLAYBOY CLUB THAT NEVER WAS

Remembering the Riverside Hotel

The first Playboy Club opened in Chicago, Illinois, in 1960, a harbinger, it was said at the time, of the upcoming Sexual Revolution. Today, many people would argue it was merely the harbinger of something absurdly tacky.

But you would need to be a complete revisionist to forget how popular these clubs once were. Montreal ended up getting the only Canadian Playboy Club in 1967, although every large Canadian city wanted one for a while. (Montreal got its Playboy Club to coincide with the opening of Expo 67.)

Ottawa newspapers printed rumours for years about a Playboy Club opening here, although it never happened. So the nation's capital had to create its own version of a Playboy Club at a place called The Rib.

A Home for "Lovely Bunnies"

Located within the Riverside Hotel on what is now River Road North in Vanier, the Rib boasted that it was Ottawa's first and "best" steakhouse. Postcards and newspaper ads touted the restaurant as the place to eat and be entertained and to be served cocktails and steaks by "lovely bunnies," just like the Playboy Club in Montreal. A discotheque could also be found at the Riverside Hotel, a popular attraction for those attending "business meetings" at the Rib.

A 1968 postcard shows Ottawa's "bunnies" as they appeared at The Riverside Hotel in Vanier.

READERS' REMARKS

I worked there the summers of '67 and '68. I was a student at Carleton at the time. The tips paid for my university education. I was also the only bunny, at least up to that time, who wore glasses. Quite an education for a farm girl from Dundas County. — *Nancy*

I was a student at St. Pat's and worked there the summer of '66. I was 15 and looked 20. My parents lived in the U.S. at the time and when they found out what my job was, they made me quit after just four weeks. — *Mary Jane*

Loved The Rib. Does anyone know what happened to one of the bunnies called Muriel who married bartender Stephen Be? — *Jacqueline*

Whatever happened to the buffet restaurant called Poppa Joe? — *Claude*

The "owner" was "Poppa Gagne." I imagine it was named after him and was much later, maybe even after the bunnies were done? — *Nancy*

Straight out of the *Mad Men* era and what looks like a set piece from the show, The Rib's atmosphere was that of "gentleman's entertainment." The restaurant was no doubt also a reliable source for the associated business-trip, expense-account receipt.

The Rib continued operations until the Riverside Hotel closed — and was later demolished in 2006 — although the bunnies had been gone for years by then.

The site of Ottawa's pseudo Playboy Club is now home to the Edgewood Care Centre. Have fun with that one.

A vintage postcard of The Rib at the Riverside Hotel. Note the "gentlemen" conducting important business meetings over cocktails and steak.

SEA MONSTERS OF THE OTTAWA RIVER

Near Arnprior, the waters of the Ottawa River widen and come to resemble more of a lake than a river, hence this stretch of the river being named Chats Lake. It reaches from the once mighty Chats Falls, now dammed for a hydro station, northwards to the rapids at Portage-du-Fort, Quebec, near Renfrew.

Bookended by these two waterfalls, this 30-km lake was the scene of much logging and timber transport during Ottawa's square timber boom of the mid-to-late 1800s. At that time, many steamships were employed to carry both crews and supplies along the river. During this period of increased steamship travel on Chats Lake, there started to be sightings of an unusual water creature of immense proportions.

Described as a large serpentine creature, a well-respected Arnprior citizen by the name of Robert Young may have been the first to report seeing the creature, telling the *Arnprior Chronicle* he had seen a monster at Chats Lake, which he described as being of enormous size and proportion.

An 1880 newspaper article from the same newspaper tells the story of a boy in a canoe encountering a serpent creature "about the size of an ordinary telegraph pole" and explained, as though stating fact, that an unknown serpent lurked in the Ottawa River, in Chats Lake.

A few years after Young's sighting, and also near Arnprior, Captain Brown of the steamship *Alliance* reported seeing a similar creature. Large. Serpentine. Fast. Then, one hot summer day in 1882, the

creature was spotted again, but this time there would be no escape for the Chats Lake Monster.

As announced in the Arnprior Chronicle on August 26, 1882, the elusive sea serpent of Chats Lake had been captured. Having struck terror in the hearts of superstitious lumbermen for decades, the capture was front-page news. It happened when the steamship *Levi Young* encountered the legendary creature of the lake.

Departing Snow Rapids, near present day Castleford, where the Bonnechere River empties into the Ottawa River, the crew of the *Levi Young* noticed a huge serpent creature swimming ahead of the boat. The newspaper article states that "Mr. John Durgan, chief engineer, and a deck hand named Shaw jumped into a boat and started in pursuit of the reptile. They succeeded in getting within striking distance of the serpent when Mr. Durgan struck it a blow over the head with his oar. This in turn enraged the creature, who churned the water into a furious froth, attacking the boat and the men inside. An oar was used to lay a powerful

rowing ashore after watching it go westward, in the direction of the Chats Falls, for some time. The men, although taken by surprise and naturally somewhat frightend, saw the serpent clearly. Mr. Williams stated to Mr. H. McLean, Warden of the County of Ottawa, in whose employ he is, and who is our informant of what is now told, that

THE SERPENT WAS DARK IN COLOR,

with body about the size of an ordinary telegraph pole, the head being somewhat smaller. It made considerable commotion in the water while swimming. He judges that it was twelve feet or more in length, although only some four or five feet of the back part of its body was visible. The number who have seen the Duchesne Lake serpent steadily increases, and some of these fine days we hope to hear of its capture. It might be mentioned that the shores on either side of the broadening river or lake

- 11-12 FOOT LENGTH
- CAPTURED IN 1882, OTTAWA RIVER

blow to the creature's neck where it writhed to rest and was then towed back to the steamship."

Once back at the ship, the crew heaved the lifeless serpent aboard the deck of the *Levi Young* where it was laid out for inspection. Aboard the ship lay a serpent creature measuring 11 feet in length and more than a foot in thickness. The jaws of the creature were pried open and measured a span of half a foot.

No further records of the creature have been found, and whatever happened to the carcass of the Chats Lake Monster remains unknown. Was it some sort of ancient fish trapped between the falls on either end of the lake after the prehistoric Champlain Sea receded? Was it an abnormally large snake, catfish or eel?

It is unclear what exactly plied the waters of the Ottawa River in those years, but there is one thing for certain — a large serpent creature was indeed captured. So as we lazily splash around at our cottages, without fear of sharks or jellyfish, remember there was once another type of creature lurking in the dark waters of the Ottawa River, a creature that could still be out there, and possibly very hungry.

The *Levi Young* was a sister ship to the *Empress*.

THE STEAMER EMPRESS.

6 THE NUCLEAR REACTOR AT TUNNEY'S PASTURE

The Tunney's Pasture federal government complex is a mix of mid-century and 1970s office buildings and towers, a sterile collection of grey concrete office buildings and black asphalt parking lots. There are no fences and little security. Not the sort of place where you would expect to find a nuclear reactor.

But Tunney's had one once. Believe it or not (apologies to Ripley's.)

According to Canadian Society For Mechanical Engineers documents, Atomic Energy Canada Limited, or AECL, placed a SLOW-POKE-2 nuclear reactor at Tunney's in 1970. The reactor was installed at 20 Goldenrod Avenue. It was constructed as a commercial testing reactor to determine its feasibility. The reactor was in full operation after it reached critical mass in 1971 and stayed at Tunney's until 1984, when it was moved to another test site in Kanata, where it was decommissioned in 1992.

The reactor, nicknamed SLOWPOKE (an acronym for Safe Low-Power Kritical Experiment) used 93 per cent enriched uranium. The core sat in a pool of regular light-water 18 feet deep, which provided cooling. The reactor at Tunney's achieved critical mass — the point at which a nuclear reaction is self-sustaining — on May 1, 1971.

The oddly shaped circular concrete bunker that remains on the shore of the Ottawa River directly opposite the old nuclear reactor site was built at the same time as the reactor in 1969-70. It was built to facilitate the increased cooling needs of Tunney's Pasture.

The pumping station bunker and pipeline were finished in 1970 and the reactor began operating a year later. Whether or not the bunker pipeline bringing cooling water to Tunney's Pasture was directly

A 1965 aerial image showing the Atomic Energy Canada Buildings at Tunney's Pasture and the area of land where the bunker and cooling water pipeline have yet to be built.

Remic Bunker

Site of nuclear reactor 1971-84

TUNNEY'S 1976

Four years after they were completed in 1976, the Remic Bunker and nuclear reactor site.

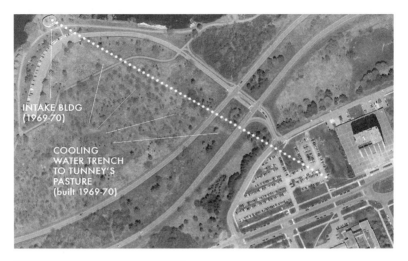

INTAKE BLDG
(1969-70)

COOLING
WATER TRENCH
TO TUNNEY'S
PASTURE
(built 1969-70)

One of the access hatches in the field along the 1970 pipeline from the bunker to Tunney's Pasture.

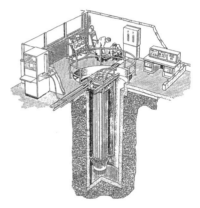

Sketch from the Canadian Society for Mechanical Engineers document of what the Tunney's Pasture nuclear reactor looked like.

related to the addition of a nuclear reactor remains speculation, but it is interesting to note the proximity and similar timeline of both projects.

You can follow the intake cooling water pipe by tracing a path that follows a series of manhole covers that lead from the river to the Tunney's Pasture site. The buildings where the nuclear reactor once existed have since been demolished, and it is currently an empty gravel parking lot.

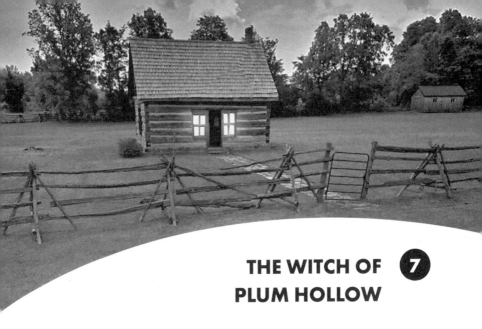

THE WITCH OF PLUM HOLLOW   **7**

South of Ottawa, just past Smiths Falls, there is a log cabin that was once home to a well known and respected witch, a woman who may have predicted John A. Macdonald becoming prime minister, and Ottawa becoming the capital of Canada.

A Witch's Tale

Jane Elizabeth Martin was born in 1794 in Cork, Ireland. Just under five-feet tall, Elizabeth was the daughter of a Spanish gypsy and a British army officer. Being the seventh daughter of a seventh daughter, Elizabeth would later claim this was the reason behind her mystical abilities.

Arranged to marry a British officer, Elizabeth was deeply in love with another man, a forbidden relationship in her family's eyes, so she and her lover fled to North America. Once on the continent, the two lovers were married and Elizabeth gave birth to a son, but their love was to be cut short with the untimely death of her husband.

The widow would soon marry a shoemaker, David Barnes, and move to a hamlet south of Smiths Falls called Sheldon's Corners. Here, the two would raise a number of children before David Barnes would suddenly leave, without explanation, in the early 1850s. Elizabeth Barnes was left with a family to take care of and no money. It was then that her mystic abilities became known to the world.

Solving Crimes and Meeting Prime Ministers

Barnes started a fortune-telling business, charging people twenty-five cents per reading. Calling herself Mother Barnes, she soon had a devoted following, and word spread of her accurate prophesies. Business was so good that in a few years she had made enough money to buy a small log cabin near Plum Hollow. It is here that her most famous sessions took place.

Upon entering the tiny cabin, visitors would go upstairs to a small room where the witch (people had begun describing Barnes that way) would be sitting at a table with some tea. Here the guest would have their fortune told in the tea leaves, a common Victorian form of fortune telling.

It was in one of these Plum Hollow sessions that Mother Barnes told police where they could find the body of Morgan Doxtader, and that it was the dead man's cousin who murdered him. The cousin was later convicted and hanged for the crime. The Witch of Plum Hollow was also known for revealing the location of buried treasure, lost personal items and, always popular, the identity of future loves.

According to lore, one of Mother Barnes early customers was a young attorney who introduced himself merely as John. He asked Mother Barnes where the capital of the soon-to-be province of Canada would be located. Gazing through time, she told the young attorney that the capital would be Bytown, and then surprised him by saying he would one day become the leader of this new province.

The man, of course, was John A. Macdonald, who did indeed become prime minster of Canada, and went on to live in the new capital, the name of which would change from Bytown to Ottawa shortly after his visit to the witch. Macdonald told the story of his visit to the "Witch of Plum Hollow" many times, the story becoming more entertaining as the years passed.

Barnes never stopped telling prophecies and worked until 1886, when she passed away at the age of 92. Originally buried in an unmarked grave, she would later receive a proper headstone, paid for by people in the area who had loved, and now missed, their neighbourhood witch.

Her original log cabin can still be found on a gravel road south of Smiths Falls called Mother Barnes Road. Previously collapsing and in disrepair, the 19th-century cabin has since been lovingly restored by its new owners.

IT HAPPENED IN CANADA

MOTHER BARNES (THE WITCH OF PLUM HOLLOW) ONE OF THE COLORFUL CHARACTERS TO BE FOUND ON THE BYWAYS OF CANADIAN HISTORY IS MOTHER BARNES. AS A FORTUNE TELLER IN THE VICINITY OF Brockville, Ont. SHE TOLD PEOPLE WITH UNCANNY ACCURACY WHERE TO FIND MISSING THINGS; WHO THEY WOULD MARRY, In 1863 SHE SOLVED THE MYSTERY SURROUNDING THE DISAPPEARANCE of ONE M. DOCKSTADER. AFTER STUDYING TEA LEAVES, SHE WAS ABLE TO TELL EXACTLY WHERE HIS BODY WOULD BE FOUND - AND IT WAS! A MAN NAMED HARTER WAS SO SHAKEN BY THIS REVELATION THAT HE CONFESSED TO MURDER AND WAS HANGED

Readers' Remarks

It's always good to remind all of us of the history in our own back yard. Please note that since the grave marker was erected, further research has shown her death was in February of 1891 (the death notice stated it was due to complications from pneumonia), which puts her date of birth closer to 1800. — Amy

I remember a story my grandfather told me of his father going to see her to get help on solving a mystery at the family farm in the Chesterville area. Let's just say, the trip was worth it. — Lyall

What a marvelous yarn. Thank you! I will hair-split a bit. She doesn't sound so much a "witch" as a seer or prophetess. — Urspo

Another great story, but I'm left wondering why did her husband leave? — Michael

He moved to Smiths Falls to open his business and hook up with another woman. — Linda

Ottawa is known at times for being overly humble, unassuming about its many achievements and historical accomplishments. It is the stiff-upper-lip bureaucrat stereotype — a city that would think it poor form to boast. As though you shouldn't proclaim to the world this is where the first electric washing machine was used or that Lorne Greene used to live on Murray Street (still proud about both.)

One of the best examples of the phenomena can be found at the corner of Bruyere Street and Sussex Drive. Here stands Mother House, the former convent for the Sisters of Charity (better known as the Grey Nuns.)

Mother House is a building few people have been inside and it is easy to miss, as there are no grand markings or architectural features, as though the Sisters did not want to detract from the majestic Notre Dame Cathedral next door. And on this unassuming building there is an innocuous, unassuming marking. When you find it, you will be staring at the second oldest sundial in North America.

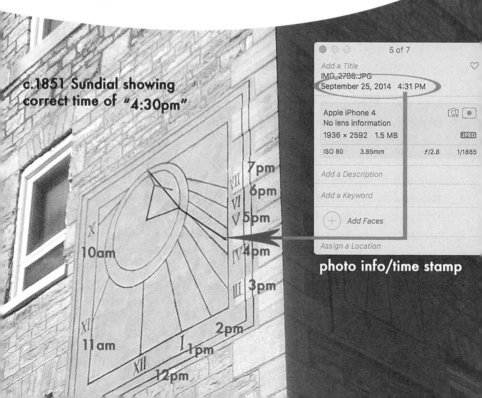

c.1851 Sundial showing correct time of "4:30pm"

photo info/time stamp

Jean-François Allard was Chaplain for the Mother House.

The Design

Ottawa's unique vertical sundials were built by Father Jean-François Allard, who had come from France to be chaplain to the Mother House. Besides being a spiritual advisor to the nuns, he was a professor of geography, geometry and mathematics with a keen interest in astronomy and the movement of the sun.

Allard soon got to work designing and building the sundials on the southwest corner of the Mother House and completed them on March 29, 1851. These became the first public timepieces in Ottawa, beating the Peace Tower by 69 years. (A sundial built in 1773 in Quebec City is the oldest on the continent.)

The two dials, 78 feet high on the west side and approximately 74 feet high on the east side, use black-painted iron "gnomons," that cast the shadow of the sun and mark the designated time carefully with Roman numerals. The western dial has hour lines from 10 a.m. to 7 p.m. and the eastern dial has hour lines from 7 a.m. to 3 p.m. These dials predate the use of time zones and show local solar time and they have been giving the correct time since 1851.

The modest timepiece (how Ottawa) sits quietly unnoticed in downtown Ottawa, continuing to give the correct time to anyone who takes the time to notice it.

9 BLAZING MAGNUMS AND STRANGE SHADOWS

Ottawa goes Hollywood (sort of)

In 1976, Ottawa had a starring role in an obscure Italian film starring Stuart Whitman. Called *Strange Shadows in an Empty Room* when it was released — which didn't seem to do the car scenes much justice — it was renamed *Blazing Magnum* by the time it hit the UK.

The film met with, uhhh, less than critical praise. The Associated Press said the plot made "little sense," and the movie would appeal only to "hardcore Eurotrash buffs." The *New York Times* may have been less kind. While noting that the Italian film had been shot in Ottawa and Montreal — and how odd was that? — the reviewer went on to say it didn't make much difference as the "camerawork was so out of focus, it may as well have been Omaha."

Ouch. See for yourself if this looks anything like Omaha, as we showcase some of the best Ottawa-shot scenes from *Blazing Shadows* in an *Empty Magnum*, or whatever this epic was called.

STUART WHITMAN JOHN SAXON MARTIN LANDAU

BLAZING MAGNUM

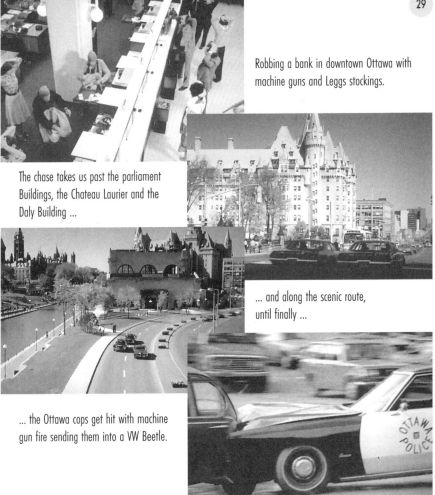

Robbing a bank in downtown Ottawa with machine guns and Leggs stockings.

The chase takes us past the parliament Buildings, the Chateau Laurier and the Daly Building ...

... and along the scenic route, until finally ...

... the Ottawa cops get hit with machine gun fire sending them into a VW Beetle.

Readers' Remarks

This film is a lot of fun. I pre-ordered the Blu-ray the second it was announced. It's a strange cross between a Poliziotteschi (crime/police drama) and a Giallo (psycho/suspense thriller) that tries to have it both ways. Hence the two titles. For an example of big studio Hollywood coming to Ottawa, check out *The Iron Curtain* starring Dana Andrews and Gene Tierney. It's the story of Igor Gouzenko's defection and features lots of Ottawa scenery. Another fun movie is *The Lost Missile of 1953*, in which our beloved Ottawa is levelled by a radioactive missile from parts unknown on its way to New York. This one stars a young Robert Loggia. — *Dwight*

I worked at Place de Ville for over ten years. No idea it was the fictional Ottawa Police Headquarters in this cool film. Nice to know! — *Holly*

Hilarious play-by-play of shots from the 70s movie shot in Ottawa. Thanks! — *Rosemary*

Being the Ill-fated Adventures of
Frederick Knapp and his Iron Tube Ship

Concealed beneath Canada's largest city lies an iron apparatus designed in Prescott, Ontario, that resembles an invention from the pages of a Jules Verne novel. A perfect example of the steampunk aesthetic, this 110-foot, ironclad, cylindrical vessel remains buried under the Gardiner Expressway, quietly resting below the traffic of thousands of commuters. Its remarkable story is one of innovation, passion and ill-fated decisions. Join me now as we uncover the where-abouts of this lost tubular dream.

Knapp's Quest

The town of Prescott sits 45 minutes south of Ottawa. During the late-19th century, it was a booming community of industry and innovation, a town that saw the inception for J.P. Wiser's Whisky and Ottawa's first railway, the Prescott & Bytown Railway. Prescott was also the terminus for the Great Lakes shipping industry and home to a Labatt brewery (which meant you were in the big leagues.) Then perhaps it should come as no

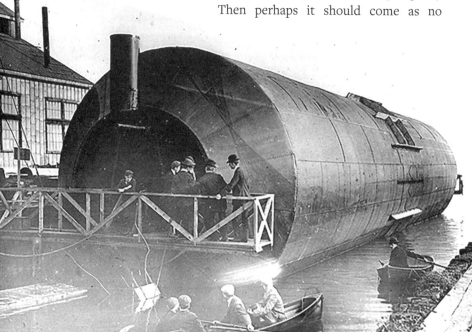

surprise that from its dusty streets would appear another creative force, an ironclad machine so imaginative, so unique and so bold that it would garner the attention of the world come 1897.

The former house of Frederick Augustus Knapp.

Queen Victoria was monarch of the British Empire at that time, but she had never visited her colonies since she hated traveling by sea. (She often got seasick.) This led one Prescott resident—who thought it was a shame the Queen had never come—on a quest to design a ship impervious to the travel and motions that causes seasickness. His name was Frederick Augustus Knapp, a lawyer turned inventor, and he designed what was probably the most bizarre, ambitious and unbelievable ship ever made.

I became fascinated with this ironclad marvel when I saw a Ripley's *Believe-It-Or-Not* illustration featuring Knapp's craft. I researched its history and was surprised to discover the tube ship was designed and briefly operated in Prescott, just a short drive from my home. I started wondering whatever happened to the ship. I now believe it lies buried under the Gardiner Expressway in downtown Toronto.

But before we get to that point, a little history on the world's only iron tube ship.

The Life and Death of the Roller Boat

Fred Knapp had a vision for a giant tube ship 800 feet long, a ship that would glide over ocean waves at 60 mph, undisturbed by the rolling sea. His idea was soon put to paper as he drew out plans for a scaled-down version of his iron dream, imagined on his many trips across the Atlantic aboard steamship liners of the day.

In an interview with the *Prescott Telegraph* in 1897, Knapp revealed he spent most of those voyages in the engine rooms of the ships,

← The Knapp roller boat moored in Toronto's harbour.

**END VIEW SHOWING INNER AND OUTER FRAME AND
INTERMEDIATE TRUSSING.**

studying the mechanics of how to overcome the resistance of water
and waves. He soon learned that a ship must not fight these elements,
but join them, and *roll* over the waves. This is what causes seasickness.

Soon after, Knapp started wondering if a ship could be built that
stayed stationary, while the waves rolled over *it*. After many years
working at a law firm in Montreal, Knapp moved back to his home-
town of Prescott, set up a law practice, purchased a home in a stone
triplex on Dibble Street and started working on his stationary ship.

I journeyed to Prescott to see if the original Knapp residence was still
there and indeed it is, 272 Dibble Street, a modest end-unit of a larger
19th-century stone triplex building. No plaque or indicator is there to tell
of what was designed behind its walls, but this is where Knapp created
what would become a most fascinating piece of nautical history.

Soon after drawing up plans for his mighty steam tube ship, Knapp
presented the concept to Polson Iron Works in Toronto and had the
company build a working scale model, nine feet in length. (The original drawings for the roller tube ship are stored in the since closed

Knapp Roller Boat.

The Knapp roller boat has been the subject of much speculation ever since its existence was made some years ago. At that time an Ottawa capitalist was backing the undertaking but the first trial did not prove much of a success and it looked very much as if the man of money would lose thirty odd thousand dollars he had invested. Since then, however, Mr. Knapp has been busily engaged perfecting the boat: not from the first did he lose faith in its practical utility as a means of overcoming many of the disadvantages of the present day navigation. All winter Mr. Knapp has been resident in Montreal or Sherbrooke, and a great deal of his time has been spent in furthering the interests of his great enterprise. That he has succeeded to some extent is apparent from the fact that a new test is to be had of the perfected boat at Prescott before a number of Montreal capitalists who have expressed interest in the craft. Recently the boat has undergone extensive alterations at its moorings in Prescott and everything is now ready for the contemplated trial, from which the inventer expects much.

KNAPP'S ROLLER BOAT ROLLS INTO THE MUD.

The Inventor Claims the Test Successful, and Will Build a Great Ocean-Going Roller.

OGDENSBURG, N. Y., Nov. 25.—Knapp's roller boat demonstrated its ability to roll to-day. In a blinding snowstorm, with a stiff north wind, it rolled from Prescott across the St. Lawrence River to Ogdensburg, but missed the channel to the upper harbor and rolled into the soft mud on a bar abreast the city, and settled hard, surrounded by snow and ice. A steamboat followed, and was unable to get near the roller, owing to shallow water.

Efforts to tow the boat by long hawsers into deep water were unsuccessful, and she may not be released until Spring. The inventor and a stockholder, who were on board, were taken off in small boats. The inventor claims success.

The boat is 110 feet long and 22 feet in diameter. An engine is suspended in a car in the centre. The motive power is applied in the form of a climbing engine. Mr. Knapp says he will now build an ocean roller boat, 800 feet long and 200 feet in diameter, with a capacity of 4,000,000 bushels of grain and a speed of twelve knots an hour

Maritime Museum of the Great Lakes in Kingston, Ontario.)

Knapp soon organized a joint stock company called The Knapp Ocean Navigation Company and raised funds from investors in Montreal, Quebec City, the UK and Toronto. His proposal to Polson Iron Works in Toronto was accepted and they were contracted to build the vessel as a working steam-powered prototype at a cost of $125,000 (in 1890 dollars).

After some trials and tests, a full-scale, 110-foot prototype was ready for launch in Toronto's harbour in June of 1899. With Knapp aboard manning the helm, the innovative new ship was to travel from Toronto to Prescott on its maiden voyage.

Perhaps because it was never officially christened or named, the poor ship was to be doomed. On June 9, it ran aground in Bowmanville, and it took a month for a tugboat to arrive and tow it all the way to Prescott where it was holed up and underwent modifications until ready for another sea trial in 1901.

Seeming to be a glutton for punishment, Knapp decided the second sea trial of the modified ship would take place on a cold February day, with a strong north wind that hampered its planned voyage across the St. Lawrence to Ogdensburg, New York.

The strong winds were no match for the very hard-to-steer giant tube ship, and Knapp and his ship ran aground on a shoal of mud off Ogdensburg, where it soon became trapped in ice and snow. A rescue team was sent out in rowboats to retrieve the passengers, who were suffering from exposure to the cold. The iron tube ship was towed back to Prescott where it remained for the winter.

Knapp decided to modify the shape of his ship into that of a giant cigar, with conical ends and a new engine, but it had to be towed to Montreal for the work. After an arduous tow and retrofit in Montreal, the roller boat was then towed back to Toronto across Lake Ontario, around Prince Edward County and into the docks of Polson Iron Works once again. There the ship sat, Knapp now out of money and investor interest, its forlorn hull left to languish in the waters off Toronto.

The orphaned vessel that no one wanted broke free of its moorings and hit another ship causing damage to both ships. The now rusting hulk was sold for scrap metal to pay for the damages. As World War I began, it was said the tubular disaster was scavenged for metal for the war effort, picked apart like a carcass under the beaks of vultures.

Left deteriorating in the shallow waters, legend says the ill-fated ship was buried under landfill in 1927, when the Toronto shoreline was expanded.

As for Knapp, he returned to Prescott, continued his law practice and dabbled in other inventions, but nothing similar to his grandiose roller boat. He died in 1942 and is buried at the Blue Church Cemetery outside of Prescott.

View of the abandoned roller ship looking west from Sherbourne Street, August 1927.

Finding the Steampunk Dream

It is remarkable how the Internet can provide a trail of bread crumbs that often leads to a successful quest. Searching records of recent archeological assessments of downtown Toronto for any mention of "Polson Iron Works," I found a 2009 report called *Toronto Transit Commission Environmental Assessments for Transit Projects in the Eastern Waterfront; Assignment 4: Stage 1; Archaeological Resource Assessment of the East Bayfront Transit Precinct City of Toronto, Ontario; Prepared for McCormick Rankin Corporation.* The report reveals the EXACT location of Knapp's Victorian tube ship. Page 21 states:

The remains of this unusual ship lie buried 356 feet (108.5m) south of the Frederick Street slip and 140 feet (42.7m) west of the Polson Iron Works dock (wharfs 35 and 36) as they existed in 1923. Today, this location corresponds to the area between Lakeshore Boulevard and the Gardiner Expressway, between Richardson and Lower Sherbourne Streets and north of the property currently known as 215 Lakeshore Boulevard East (Figure A 13). Placement of the vessel under these roads is generally consistent with that proposed earlier by Stinson and Moir (1991:112)

Apparently, according to the archeological assessment, in 1923 soundings were done by the Toronto Harbour Commission that labeled a "wrecked roller boat" and that no dredging was to be done here. This means the remains of the tubular ship were likely covered over by fill as the land was extended, and it remains buried there to this day.

Using Google Maps with the corresponding archeological survey plans, we can see that the ship lies buried perpendicular to Lake Shore Blvd, and partially underneath the Gardiner Expressway, behind what is now a FedEx depot.

Whether this unusual chapter in maritime engineering warrants a proper archeological excavation to find a 19th-century ironclad tube ship is a matter left to city officials, but next time you pass behind that FedEx depot on Lakeshore Boulevard East, remember the steampunk dream that lies below.

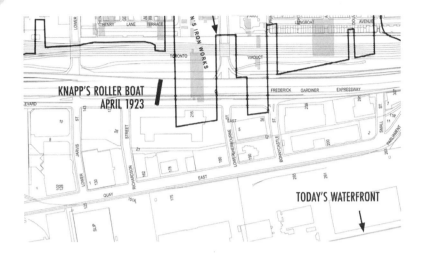

KNAPP'S ROLLER BOAT
APRIL 1923

TODAY'S WATERFRONT

Site where the roller ship is buried near the Toronto waterfront.

Ghost roller boat, Lakeshore Boulevard, Toronto, looking east.

AN OTTAWA UNDERGROUND TUNNEL

Before security and safety became of such paramount importance to so many, Ottawa had a number of publicly accessible underground tunnels. The tunnels allowed residents to escape the frigid winter temperatures and move about in — if not warmth — then certainly a greater degree of comfort.

The most famous of these underground tunnels is probably the one that linked the Chateau Laurier with the old Union Station, once connecting train passengers to the hotel without anyone ever needing to step outside. Closed to the public, this tunnel will most likely stay that way for a long time, now that the old train station has become the temporary home to the Senate.

A lesser-known tunnel under Ottawa is the sealed mid-century tunnel that once connected Freiman's department store (now Hudson's Bay) to the store's parkade facility on George Street. This tunnel was closed sometime in the early 2000s but I was fortunate enough to record the tunnel on video back in 1999 when I filmed a chase scene for a short film I was working on.

Having recently stumbled across the closed-off entrance while in the basement of the Bay looking to buy a woolen blanket to escape

The former Freiman's parkade where the subterranean tunnel was accessed.

Readers' Remarks

There is another tunnel between the West Bloc and the Centre Bloc of Parliament only opened to parliamentarians and clad in white marble. — *Larry*

And one crossing the street between 180 Wellington and West block. — *Dan*

I remember there was a malted milk bar just inside the old Freiman's as you left the tunnel. I also suspect that one of the reasons the tunnel was closed was to combat shoplifting. I remember hearing the staff talk about how they often chased people through the tunnels with piles of clothes in their arms. — *Brian*

I remember using that tunnel as a kid in the 70s and 80s. And the malt shop in the basement of the Bay. — *Bryan*

As a kid, my mom would park there and we would use the tunnel. Back then, there was clear glass where the middle red squares are, and a conveyor belt. You paid for your merchandise and they would put it on the belt so you wouldn't have to carry it. You would walk beside it and watch it make its way to the garage. — *Mich*

the cold, I was reminded to dig out the old VHS tape that documented this tunnel.

These photos are from that short film and I can see now that the tunnel is actually a phenomenal piece of mid-century architecture, utilizing materials and an aesthetic that provides a unique glimpse back to mid-century shopping conveniences. It resembles a colourful set piece from the TV show *Mad Men*.

A Little History

The tunnel dates from November 4, 1959, when Freiman's opened their "ultra modern" parkade on George Street, a Guggenheim-museum-inspired spiral parking garage that linked to their store across the street

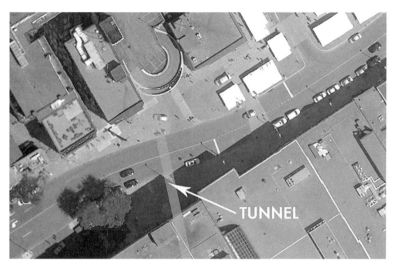

Tunnel route from the parkade to The Bay.

by means of an air-conditioned — and heated — tunnel.

In a ribbon-cutting ceremony that brought out the mayor and other community leaders, the guests toured the 231-foot tunnel, taking in the glazed subway tiles and the kaleidoscope of coloured acrylic panels that also acted as storage compartments for the store's seasonal decorations.

After Freiman's was bought by the Bay in 1972, the tunnel remained opened and in service until sometime in the early 2000s. I'm thinking 9-11 likely forced it to close.

The Bay has closed off the tunnel entrance and now uses the area for storage. The entrance from the parkade side has also been sealed and locked. But from the Bay side, the original 1959 illuminated sign can still be seen.

The now sealed entrance to the tunnel.

⑫ DOING THE HOKEY POKEY

In 1916 the consumption of alcohol in Ontario became illegal. In 1920, the United States passed similar legislation and the Era of Prohibition began.

As we all know, prohibition turned out to be less than a rousing success and both countries would repel its ban on alcohol before the end of the decade. Until that happened, though, moonshiners and bootleggers had a fun time.

Some of the most successful bootleggers of the prohibition era came from the Ottawa area. Folklore has it that bootleggers ran a hidden distillery in the woods near Prescott by a railway line to the United States, and they produced what was to become a favourite drink of the Roaring Twenties — pokey moonshine.

The pokey moonshine distillery brought notoriety to Ottawa and even led to a visit by J. Edgar Hoover, the first director of the Federal Bureau of Investigation. If Hoover was looking for the pokey moonshine still, he never found it. *Ottawa Rewind* has (we believe).

Still with Us

Moonshine is a slang term for high-proof distilled spirits produced illicitly without government authorization under the darkness of night, under the moon, if you will. The quality of moonshine changed from still to still, region to region, as did the brand names. Ottawa's moonshine was called pokey moonshine, for reasons that are unclear to us today (and were perhaps even unclear at the time).

The "pokey moonshine" would be crated as "tea" according to local lore, before being loaded onto the CPR train from Ottawa bound for Prescott, then over to Ogdensburg, New York.

A newspaper article from 1928 describes a settlement south of the city of Ottawa as being a good place for "pokey moonshine." The newspaper articled placed the settlement near the St. Lawrence and Ottawa Railway line, which ran from Prescott to Ottawa.

According to a great post on Al Lewis's *Bytown.net* site, there was a still built off these tracks where pokey moonshine was manufactured, bottled and then packaged into wooden crates labelled "tea."

It is unclear what would happen next. Did the moonshiners pay the train engineer to stop the train by the still? Was there a scheduled stop where they would sneak the whisky onto the train? However, it worked, the moonshine made its way to the Prescott piers, where it was loaded onto boats and shipped across the St. Lawrence to the United States, most of it making its way to New York City.

J. Edgar Hoover

In 1920 the United States created the Bureau of Prohibition, a federal law enforcement agency given the task of enforcing the new ban on alcohol. In the beginning it was a branch of the Bureau of Internal Revenue, although it soon morphed into its own agency with a new name: the Federal Bureau of Investigation.

↖ A typical forest whiskey still for making moonshine.

J Edgar Hoover's G-men at work   ... and the man himself.

In 1924, the United States Attorney General made J. Edgar Hoover the acting director of the FBI. Shortly after he was appointed, Hoover made a visit to Prescott, where he had a cousin living in the area. Whatever the reason for the visit, it is said Hoover and his cousin spent several days driving around the woods south of Ottawa, as though searching for something.

If Hoover was searching for the pokey moonshine distillery, which he almost certainly would have known about, he never found it. *Ottawa Rewind* may have had better luck.

Discovering a Backwoods Still

Using old maps and newspaper articles of the day, I went searching along the old St. Lawrence and Ottawa Railway line for the prohibition-era distillery. I soon found a rusty metal gate. Overgrown, the

gate lead to a pathway into the woods that seemed worthy of further exploration. Following the overgrown path into the woods the ruins of an old log cabin soon became visible.

The log walls had crumbled away and now lay rotting, but the crude stone foundation could still be seen, as well as various metal vessels and pots that could have been used in the distilling process.

Sections of long collapsed tin roofing were strewn around the site that made me suspect that this was indeed the location of the fabled pokey moonshine still.

Taking a moment to reflect on how this parcel of land may have looked during the prohibition era, I could almost hear the sounds of the men and women hard at work making illegal whisky, bottling and crating it in "tea" crates, the sound of a distant steam whistle coming from a train bound for Prescott.

Such a unique part of Ottawa history should be preserved and that is why I am keeping its location a secret. Perhaps I am completely wrong and it is not the old pokey moonshine still. But I have learned through past adventures to trust my gut, and I believe the photos you are looking at show what is left of the Ottawa moonshine still that J. Edgar Hoover never found.

You put your right foot out,
You put your right foot in,
And you shake it all about.
You do the Hokey Pokey,
And you turn it all around,
That's what it's all about.

13 THAT TIME WE HAD A KENNY ROGERS ROASTERS RESTAURANT

A recent trip down memory lane had me thinking of the time I pulled into a strip mall off Bank Street in the mid-'90s to try a new restaurant called Kenny Rogers Roasters. Yes, that Kenny Rogers, the country music star that knew when to hold them and when to fold them.

Now, Ottawa in the mid-'90s was something of a culinary wasteland, with Lick's burgers on Bank Street being a big deal because they sang your food order, and the Keg being considered the high end of high-end restaurants. There really wasn't much to choose from on a Friday night for a dinner out when I was in my early twenties. One night though, I saw Kenny's emblazoned head on an illuminated sign and I was drawn to his rotisserie chicken palace as though hypnotized. It turned out to be one of the most memorable food experiences of my life.

You see, before hipster restaurants started serving drinks in mason jars and food on a live-edge wooden plank, Kenny Rogers was opening restaurants across the globe that served down-home food on a metal tray, an ambience that was reminiscent of an army mess hall or upscale penitentiary. After entering the welcoming doors of the majestic Kenny Rogers Roasters at 2629 Alta Vista Road, you were greeted by a delightful hostess that handed you a tray with those sectioned off areas to dump in your food. It was glorious.

Rewinding back to 1991, country musician Kenny Rogers and former KFC CEO John Y. Brown Jr., former governor of the U.S. state of Kentucky, opened a chain of restaurants that had a menu centred on wood-fired rotisserie chicken. The chain eventually grew to over 350 restaurants, including locations in Canada, the Middle East and Asia.

Ottawa was lucky enough to receive a location in the Alta Vista Plaza off Bank Street. Alas, the Kenny Rogers culinary experience would only be available to the Ottawa masses for a few short years. A flaming nova, if you will, it is remembered by many today for no more reason than a classic episode of Seinfeld, featuring Kramer's love of the restaurant chain.

No wonder Kramer was smitten. Kenny's place was clean and well appointed, with various Kenny Rogers' photos and paraphernalia, and I gotta say,

Kenny Rogers singing for his supper.

Menu : Kenny's Greatest Meal

Pasta is great source of carbohydrate. Did you know that carbohydrate 'feed' the brain and provide sustained energy?

Beef Bolognaise

Macaroni & Cheese

Cheesy Chicken

Vegetable Fusion

pretty good food for a chain restaurant. That's why it was with great surprise I learned in 1998 that Kenny Rogers Roasters had entered Chapter 11 bankruptcy. It was later sold to Nathan's Famous, Inc. for $1.25 million USD, the deal closing on April 1, 1999 (April Fool's Day.) The Kenny Rogers Roasters in Ottawa closed the same year.

Nathan's Famous later sold the chain to their Asian franchiser, Roasters Asia Pacific (Cayman) Limited, and the very last Kenny Rogers Roasters that operated in North America closed on December 31, 2011.

But it's hard to keep Kenny Rogers down. To this day the chain is HUGE in Asia, where it flourishes under the ownership of Berjaya Group, gambling and winning with almost 140 restaurants and expansion plans to enter Malaysia and the Philippines. Pacific islands in the stream of rotisserie chicken sauce, if you will.

Ottawa's Kenny Rogers Roasters is now a Cora's restaurant, but no matter how hard they try to camouflage the building, its distinctive architectural details reveal its roots as an illustrious Kenny Rogers Roasters. A restaurant that I wish could have found a way to hold them, and never fold.

Kramer in a fit of Kenny Rogers Roasters delirium.

A CHRISTMAS MYSTERY
The disappearance of Rockcliffe's Flying Fortress

In October 1943, Rockcliffe Air Base became home to the 168th Heavy Transport Squadron (HTS), a squadron formed that same year to handle the large quantity of mail destined for military personnel serving in Europe and North Africa. Rockcliffe soon became the central hub for mail from across Canada on its way to troops and service personnel overseas. Love letters, family correspondence, birthday and holiday gifts as well as freight were all transported to the men and women far from home, boosting morale and keeping them connected to loved ones back home.

On December 15 1944, one of the six B-17 Flying Fortresses that made up the 168th HTS — a bomber with the serial number B17-9203 — had just delivered a load of Christmas mail to Canadian troops serving in North Africa, where the Royal Canadian Air Force had a base in Morocco.

On December 15, 1944, the aging B-17 Flying Fortress that had made the trip from Ottawa to Morocco was loaded with return mail. It took off for the nation's capital with Pilot Horace Hillcoat and a crew of eight. They were all looking forward to returning home with their precious Christmas cargo.

Throttling up the four radial engines of the B-17, Hillcoat lifted the mailbird into the Moroccan skies, heading for the Azores, a small group of islands in the North Atlantic Ocean. After a brief stop there, Hillcoat would then fly on to Newfoundland, before reaching his final destination at Rockcliffe.

Leaving the African shoreline, Hillcoat took the B-17 across the Atlantic Ocean, headed for the island airstrip some 1,500 km away. He and his crew were never seen again.

When contact was lost with Hillcoat's B-17, a search and rescue mission scoured the area where the plane may have disappeared. Some mailbags were found floating on the surface of the ocean, but there were no other signs of wreckage or debris. No distress call was made before the plane disappeared. It simply vanished. Hillcoat and the crew were soon classified as "missing."

Over the years, there have been many theories on what might have happened to the flight. Was Hillcoat and his crew ambushed by an attacking German Luftwaffe aircraft, sending them to a watery grave? Did the well-used B17 (all the planes had been purchased from the U.S. Air Force) suffer a mechanical malfunction?

Another theory is that the ill-fated B-17 was shot down by the anti-aircraft guns of a German U-boat. A number of German U-boats

The mail room at Rockcliffe Air base, circa 1944.

STAR WEEKLY TORONTO NOVEMBER 27, 1943 **10** CENTS

Star Weekly, November 27, 1943.

Readers' Remarks

I am the grandson of H.B. Hillcoat. Thank you for sharing this account of the events that led to his disappearance/ death. My mother was about 3 years old and my grandmother was pregnant with my aunt when this tragedy occurred. Both daughters grew up to be fine women. — *Travis*

Great bit of history. I like the site. It is fantastic to read about the history of Ottawa. As I drove street cars in Ottawa as well as buses, it would be nice to see some history of those days on street cars as well as buses if you have any history of them. I am eighty years old. — *Jeff*

Great article. Sad but a great article. — *Jim*

shot down Allied aircraft in the vicinity of the Azores, a fate that could have taken down Hillcoat's aircraft.

In return, numerous U-boats were sunk by Allied anti-submarine patrols in the same area. It is quite possible Hillcoat's B-17 was shot down by one of these sunken U-boats, the story disappearing along with the doomed German crew.

A December 21, 1944, newspaper clipping reported on the missing plane and gave a list of the crew. It turned out that only Pilot Horace Hillcoat was from Ottawa. He and his wife lived on Kirkwood Avenue in Westboro, and the house is still there today.

The crew of that ill-fated plane is still classified as "missing," and are among hundreds of other missing aircrew from World War II on the Commonwealth Aircrew Memorial on Sussex Drive. The disappearance of the Christmas Flying Fortress is an enduring mystery that may never be solved.

⑮ OTTAWA, PLANET X AND THE DOOMSDAY PROPHECY

In 1924, an event occurred at Ottawa's Dominion Observatory that played an instrumental role in what would later be the discovery of the dwarf planet Pluto.

Now quietly hidden off Carling Avenue, the Dominion Observatory once sat on the outskirts of the city, far from the bright lights of downtown. Its huge copper dome once retracted to reveal a giant telescope that scanned the heavens for new planets.

Looking like some lost relic from a Jules Verne novel, this unique Ottawa building is where two astronomers accidentally discovered what would later be known as Planet X. Or as some call it today: The Doomsday Planet.

The Heavens and the Hell

Scanning an old newspaper article from a 1930 Ottawa Journal, I found a curious headline: "Pluto's major role had its setting in the Dominion Observatory at Ottawa."

This piqued my interest, and after further research I discovered Ottawa's observatory was part of a curious investigation known in astronomy circles of the day as "The Ottawa Object." The investigation began one night in 1924 when two astronomers working at the Dominion Observatory — Francois Henroteau and "girl astonomer"

M.S. Burland — discovered a mysterious planet they would come to call "Planet X."

It would be six years until their discovery was publicized, though, and then only as part of a larger scientific report on the discovery of Pluto. The Ottawa Observatory director at the time, R.M. Stewart, announced that the mysterious object had been found during a search for pre-discovery observations of Pluto by Henroteau and Miss Burland on photo plates taken here in Ottawa in 1924. The director remarked that the "orbit of the unusual object is uncertain."

Ottawa Journal, April 30, 1930.

CAPTION READS: A heavenly drama in which a girl astronomer played a major role had its setting in the Dominion observatory at Ottawa. Information received from Harvard college observatory led Dominion authorities to believe planet photographed by them in 1924 was new planet and not the planet "X" reported from Lowell, Mass. Study of photographic plates and the discovery of the minute speck strengthened supposition. (I) Miss M. S. Burland. young astronomer, who discovered tiny speck of supposed new planet on photographic plate. (2) Photograph of planet. (3) Meldrum R. Stewart, director of Dominion observatory, under whose direction search for planet was made. (4) Diagram showing position of supposed new planet in universe. (5) The telescope in the dome of the Dominion observatory. The short cylinder to the right is the camera, which took the photograph. A clockwork attachment to the telescope revolved it to offset the motion of the earth, and (6) Dr. Francois Henroteau. the Belgian-born astronomer of the Dominion observatory, who took the original photograph.

The Ottawa Object plates were subsequently lost, and no one could find the planet again, although many people tried over the years. For many years, there were widespread doubts (or outright chuckling) surrounding the Ottawa Object.

That changed in 2016 when two scientists with the California Institute of Technology published a paper stating a Neptune-sized planet does indeed exist in the outer limits beyond Pluto.

Konstantin Batygin and Mike Brown said the planet orbits the sun every 15,000 years. They said 4.5 million years ago the giant planet was knocked out of the planet-forming region near the sun, and settled into a "distant elliptical orbit," where it may again return into our solar system, potentially smashing into the Earth, or coming terrifyingly close to it.

This news forced one more change to the name of our mysterious planet. From Planet X, to The Ottawa Object, it is now called, by some: The Doomsday Planet.

And to think it all started on a quiet street off Carling Avenue.

A 15 inch telescope like the one that was at the Ottawa Observatory. (photo: Royal Astronomical Society)

THE LOST VILLAGE OF TONIATA

New France, Flea Markets and a Missing Iroquois Town

Sometime in the 1700s, a village marked prominently on maps as being located somewhere along the St. Lawrence River between Prescott and Gananoque disappeared from history.

This mysterious village has vanished from all records, its whereabouts unknown. Having been a significant enough settlement to be noted by explorers and mapmakers, what happened to it and why did it vanish from the landscape and all future maps?

Using clues left behind in centuries-old records, we will try to piece together what happened to this village and finally pinpoint its exact location.

The Search for Toniata

Flea markets are always a great place to pick up cool pieces of nostalgia and things you'd never find in a regular shopping mall. Attending one such flea market a few years ago, I saw a vendor pull out an old, framed map and ask his neighbour what kind of price he should put on it. I quickly offered the contents of my wallet, which was $60. I got the map!

I left the flea market with an almost 300-year-old map of the St. Lawrence River, Ottawa River and Lake Ontario. Dated 1757, the map was a stunning example of this country's early explorations and mapmaking. Pouring over this incredible record from the age of exploration in Canada, I noticed many recognizable villages and settlements, but one stood out as something strange, a place called Toniata.

Bought for $60 at a flea market, this 1757 French map shows a mysterious village called "Toniata."

Shown as somewhere between Prescott and Gananoque on the north shore of the St. Lawrence, this village is clearly marked but I had never heard of such a place. Where did it go? A quick Google search revealed that this is regarded as "one of the great mysteries of early Canadian history." No one has been able to provide "the identification of the site of a First Nations village or camp known as Toniata."

A school in Brockville is named after this mystery village, and its website clearly notes the oddity:

From Champlain's exploration of the Upper St. Lawrence, until the British captured Quebec, maps showed a spot named Toniata. This area was defined as being placed halfway between present day Ogdensburg and the Gananoque

Toniata clearly marked as "Village Of Iroquois" on this map by John Mitchell "Map of The British and French Dominions in North America" circa 1757.

River. The name, which had various spellings on the old French maps, seemed to disappear as the British maps replaced the French maps.

Checking my own collection of old map references, Toniata appears on most 17th-century French maps, with variations in spelling. Some maps call it "Tonthata", others, "Toniata." One map calls it "Toniata Village of The Iroquois." Further research revealed that there is an account called *Memoir Upon the Late War in North America, Between the French and English, 1755-60: Followed by Observations Upon the Theatre of Actual War, and by New Details Concerning the Manners and Customs of the Indians: with Topographical Maps, Volume 2* by Pierre Pouchot, January 1, 1866 that describes how Toniata was south of La Galette, or what is now Prescott, and how Toniata was a very distinct place of reference.

In 1654, Père Simon le Moyne, a Jesuit priest, made the first recorded voyage of a European through the upper

READERS' REMARKS

A marvellous tale. I so enjoy these. I collect legendary and mythical names for my fantasy map. I may include this one as it fits my fancy. — *Urspo*

Thank you, another well researched, great story. I'm surprised there hasn't been any on-the-ground research. — *Steve*

I always look forward to your stories of lost places in time. I will think of the Village of Toniata each time I drive on the 401. Maybe this story will spur an interest for archeologists to explore this area and see what they can recover from the past. — *Catherine*

Fascinating. I am now engaged in some research about French and Indian settlement as a result of helping a chum with his own family history research, and this is a part of history I sure didn't know much about before. Wonderful story. — *Brenda*

Thank you for your work in bringing to light the past of our area. It really is amazing the information that is there if you just connect the dots. I hope that the area of Toniata is investigated further so we may know more about the people. — *Rosemary*

I would imagine that maps from the 1920s to 1940s might show the remains of Yonge Mills. — *Scott*

Well done, I loved the article. My experience with old maps is that proportions are often way off. It is hard to measure distances by canoe or on foot in the woods, today, or 400 years ago. The term "league" was not a well defined unit of distance either. — *Steven*

Toniata was one of the borders/boundaries of the infamous Crawford Treaty of 1783, the land treaty which was signed in Kingston and included the section of Eastern Ontario (including the parliament buildings) about which is still disputed today. — *John*

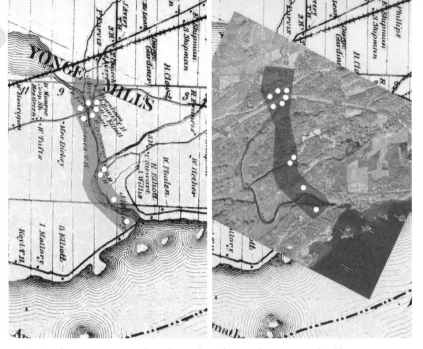

LEFT: Overlaying a current map shows the river has either moved its course, or the old map was inaccurate. Note the 401 highway now goes through the old village of Yonge Mills. RIGHT: Yonge Mills was a village built on Jones Creek, formerly Toniata River. Mills and other structures are indicatred by dots along the river.

St. Lawrence. He was sent from Montreal to establish a mission at Oswego, New York. Along the way, he stopped at the village of Toniata where he observed native Indians fishing for eel.

Further research shows there was once a body of water called "Toniata River." This river could be an important clue in locating the lost village, yet no rivers are called Toniata today. It seems likely that its name was changed from "Toniata River" to "Jones Creek" after the British arrived in the 1700s. When the French arrived to the Thousand Islands region in the mid-1600s, they named the small river Toniata River, and located it near the village of Toniata. The French described a village of Indigenous peoples in an area of eight miles adjacent to what became Jones Creek.

So, now we have a good clue to follow. To find the lost village, we just need to find Jones Creek. A visit to Google Maps and the McGill Digital Historical Atlas reveals a likely location.

It seems in the 1700s and 1800s, the Toniata River, or Jones Creek, was settled by Loyalists and made into a milling village known as "Yonge Mills." Saw mills, gristmills, a hotel and homes all dotted the area until it also faded from history. The 401 Highway was built through the village and nothing now remains of Yonge Mills.

This is likely the spot of the original lost village—a quiet river meeting the larger St. Lawrence River. As often happens in history, an original village is built upon by future inhabitants at a place of strategic and economic importance.

This place is situated on a high rocky plateau on the northeast side of the creek where it commands an impressive view down the mighty St. Lawrence in both directions, a necessary and common defensive trait for any village of that era. Our lost village has likely never been found because the area where it is located is an area of undeveloped land, an unexplored area of dense woods.

A small road, Sherwood Springs Road, winds past where the village of Toniata likely stood 400 years ago, all evidence of its bustling happenings lost in time under the leaves and grasses of nature.

Perhaps we should let this centuries-old village remain quietly hidden, its secrets buried for eternity. Or maybe Canadian archeologists would like to explore and unearth its remains, revealing more about early St. Lawrence Iroquois history, a chapter in time that has eluded much study. Until, possibly, now.

The areas shaded in red are where I believe the lost village of Toniata lies.

⑰ HISTORY AT A BUSY INTERSECTION

I was a passenger in a car driving west along Riverside Drive one day, when it stopped at traffic lights. I noticed by the side of the road a wall of old stone. A faded plaque was mounted on it, but before I could notice much more the light turned green and we drove away.

What was that mysterious stonewall, right by the side of a road that is used by tens-of-thousands of motorists each day? A quick Google Streetview visit revealed it was a "Frankensteined" wall, a wall hobbled together by the National Capital Commission (NCC) from the ruins of a cabin built by one of Ottawa's first settlers: Braddish Billings.

We Began with Ira and Braddish

The first settler of European descent to build a permanent home in our region was Philemon Wright, an American who came in 1800 and settled on the Quebec side of the river. In 1810 Ira Honeywell built a log cabin in Nepean. Nothing remains of this cabin, just an NCC plaque off Woodroffe Avenue near the Ottawa River that tells you Honeywell's cabin was once nearby.

Next to arrive on the Ontario side of the river was Braddish Billings, who built a cabin in 1812 at what is now the intersection of Bank Street and Riverside Drive. Billings made his cabin of round logs with no windows. He likely was attracted to the riverfront site because of its close proximity to the Rideau River, its abundant timber, its creek, and its fertile soil.

↑ The Billings cabin with stone chimney beside Riverside Dr. during a 1900 flood of the Rideau River.

He built a sawmill and began clearing the land, planting potatoes, hay, corn and turnips. He also continued lumbering for Philemon Wright. His ventures proved successful and in 1829 he built a substantial estate on the hill above his original cabin, what we now know as the Billings Estate Museum, owned and operated by the City Of Ottawa.

With his new estate house, the original cabin Billings built in 1812 fell into disrepair. A Methodist church was constructed next to the cabin, a wooden structure that remained until 1960, when the NCC tore down the church and cabin in order to widen Riverside Drive. Taking stones from the demolition, they built a small wall, which is what I saw by the side of the road.

If you are driving down Riverside heading west (you can't see it if you are heading east) or if you are travelling on the path along the east bank of the river, take a moment to observe what remains of one of Ottawa's oldest structures.

Readers' Remarks

Thanks for researching this.
I've never noticed that structure, but will make a bike trip over there to see it for myself. It's unfortunate that the city saw no significance to this and other historical buildings at the time it was demolished. — *Joel*

Always another interesting bit of Ottawa history to learn about. At least the NCC kept the stones and made a plaque to mark the first settler Billings's cabin. — *Cathy*

I have seen that structure 1,000 times and did not know what it was. Typical Ottawa, doing something like this. They stifle or dump huge amounts on other obscure sites. Thank you for clearing up "the wall." — *John*

I imagine the Billings sawmill location might have become lost with the NCC work. I tried the site geoOttawa.com but (the sawmill) no longer exists. — *Richard*

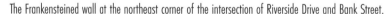

The Frankensteined wall at the northeast corner of the intersection of Riverside Drive and Bank Street.

⑱ OTTAWA'S FORGOTTEN MOVIE THEATRE

There once was a time when it seemed a movie theatre could be found on every street corner in downtown Ottawa. The majority of those old theatres have been torn down, replaced by more lucrative office and retail space. A few remain as repertoire theatres, such as the well preserved and vibrant Bytowne and Mayfair theatres

There is, however, another theatre that remains intact, sitting vacant and abandoned for more than twenty years, concealed from view behind a facade of government offices. This shuttered 1,200-seat theatre would be one of the largest in the city were it still open. It is the former Place De Ville Cinema located at 300 Sparks Street.

The Place of the City

Opened by Famous Players, Place de Ville Cinema opened on April 1, 1971, and was one of the few piggyback cinemas in Canada. It was part of an ambitious plan by developer Robert Campeau to regenerate the downtown core with a massive shopping, retail and office district utilizing the most modern of 1970s amenities.

For almost a century the area had been home to the city's streetcar garages, but when the streetcars stopped running in 1959, Campeau purchased the land. He constructed office towers on the site that he named A, B, and C, along with the Podium Building, two large hotels — the

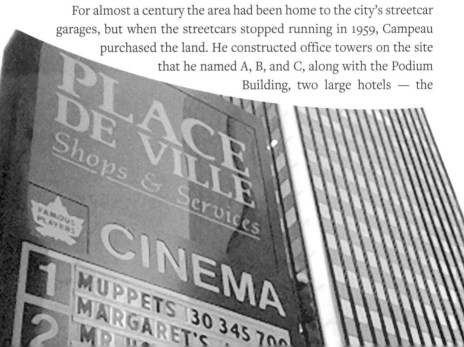

The Podium Building designed by Robert Campeau.

Ottawa Delta City Centre (411 rooms) and the Ottawa Marriott (487 rooms) — as well as the city's largest underground parking garage with space for 974 cars. Within this complex he also constructed the Place de Ville Cinema.

The theatre was hidden from view, surrounded by office space in the Podium Building, a four-storey building between the Marriott Hotel and Lyon Street. It was essentially a giant concrete box in the middle of the building. The two cinemas were stacked on top of one another, with a massive lobby and escalators to take customers from one level to another.

Lush carpeting and the latest in cinema technology were incorporated into the new

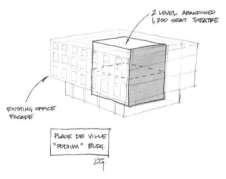

2 LEVEL ABANDONED 1,200 SEAT THEATRE

EXISTING OFFICE FACADE

PLACE DE VILLE "PODIUM" BLDG.

The hidden entrance to the Place de Ville Cinema.

theatre. A special elevator was installed for the projectionist to travel from one cinema to the other. Cinema 1 boasted 751 seats and Cinema 2 had 437 seats for a total of 1,228 seats.

Cinema 1 alone would be the largest downtown movie theatre in Ottawa, were it still open. For comparison, the Bytowne has 650 seats and the Mayfair has 325.

It Ended with Muppets

After its grand opening — showing *Little Big Man* and *Love and Other Strangers* — the Place de Ville Cinemas would operate until 1996, finally closing its doors on March 18 of that year. The final movies shown were *Mr. Holland's Opus* and *Muppet Treasure Island*.

In 25 years of operation, that theatre saw some notable figures pass through its doors. Former Prime Minister Pierre Trudeau lined up to see *The Godfather* in 1972. Singer Tom Jones didn't line up when he performed in Ottawa in 1972. He bought every ticket to a matinee screening in Cinema 1, so he could watch the *Godfather* alone.

Even when it was open, the Place de Ville theatre was hard to find, hidden within the Podium building, so finding it today proved even more difficult, but it is still there, as these photos show.

A recent drive along the 401 Highway brought back memories of the same trip 30 years earlier with my family in our little Volkswagen Beetle. Like most family road trips in the late '70s, we'd stop at one of the rest stops along the 401 to go to the bathroom, grab a bite to eat and fuel up the tank. Spending less than a few minutes at these rest stops, I now think I took for granted what is now a remarkable piece of lost architecture.

My recollection of these rest stops was that they all had a unique dome-shaped roof that made them look a little like spaceships. At the time, that didn't interest me as much as the green Jello in the glass display cases by the front door. But with fond memories of those restaurants, I set out to revisit one of them during my recent drive, only to discover I couldn't. They had all been demolished and replaced with ONroute rest stops.

When I got home and did some research, I discovered there is little record of these once grand domed rest stops. But I did manage to find some background info on what I think was an important part of our Canadian culture and a unique architectural icon.

The Kohl Flying Restaurant

Looking like a landed UFO, these unusual rest stops were designed by Toronto architect Harry B. Kohl. Kohl was one of the premier architects of the 1960s, having designed cutting-edge, prefab model homes for the National Home Show. After graduating from the University of Toronto in 1947, Kohl designed a

Khol's designs incorporated geodesic domes into the ceilings of rest stops.

number of homes, apartment towers, and eventually, the Millhaven maximum security penitentiary. Kohl died in 1973, but many of his designs still live on in the Greater Toronto Area.

Kohl was into geodesic domes, which he incorporated into his design for the 401 rest stops, a contract he was awarded in the early 1960s when the 401 highway system was being built. Kohl believed circular shapes accommodated the circulation of people better than square shapes, and his designs, including the 401 rest stops, reflect this theory.

Built of wood and stone in typical mid-century modern fashion, Kohl designed his rest stops with a domed red roof that included a tall spire to catch the attention of passing motorists. Teaming up with the Texaco Oil Company, Kohl's rest stops were completed in 1962 and usually contained a restaurant that was either an independent diner with typical 1960s decor, or a Scott's Chicken Villa Kentucky Fried

↻ A 1960s postcard of Kohl's domed spaceship rest stop in Woodstock, Ontario. BELOW: Detail of stonework on Kohl's rest stop.

In 2009, the Woodstock rest stop looks nothing like its original 1962 incarnation.

Chicken, as was the case at the Kingston, Port Hope and Woodstock locations.

I remember pulling up to Kohl's domed masterpieces as a kid in the back of the family car and being in awe of the futuristic, space-age design and its fascinating exposed geodesic dome above the restaurant, as I sat below eating my Jello and greasy burger.

When I grew up and moved to Ottawa, I still stopped into these domed stations on my way home or on road trips to Toronto, but they evolved over time and were drastically altered to try and keep up with more modern design trends.

The original spires were removed. The dome was painted brown. The covered breezeway from the gas station was removed, and the independent restaurants were replaced with fast food chains.

Eventually, the Kohl stations began to be demolished in the early 2000s to make way for ONroute stations. Google Streetviews still show the Kohl rest stops from its 2009 streetview photo collection, but there are none left today.

Readers' Remarks

What I do remember of these stops on the 401, besides the architecture, was the food menu and how heavy it was compared with today's taste. Full roast beef dinners or roast turkey with all the fixings, plus big desserts, often cakes and ice cream. I wonder how anyone could then drive for hours on end on the 401 without falling asleep at the wheel.— *Larry*

I had almost forgotten about these cool Jetson-like rest stops. They were a part of my childhood road trip memories too — though we wouldn't actually eat in one. My mom always made a picnic to save money. Sad they are gone. — *Lara*

I remember the restaurants fondly. The one in Odessa opened while I was in high school. It used to be called the Chatelaine — I have found a photo with it named the Bon Voyage. It was not an official 401 rest stop. The one on the 401 between Odessa and Kingston was a Scott's restaurant. — *Corry*

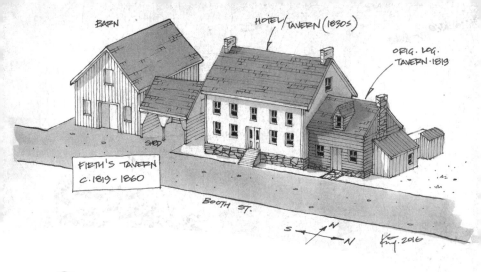

BARN

HOTEL/TAVERN (1830S)

ORIG. LOG. TAVERN · 1819

SHED

FIRTH'S TAVERN C. 1819 - 1860

BOOTH ST.

Kng. 2016

(20) OTTAWA'S FIRST PUB

Surprise! It Wasn't Irish

When it was called Bytown, this city had a legendary place of great merriment, a place where thirsty canal labourers, raftsmen and travelers could gather to relax and have fun. It was Ottawa's first pub, a place called Mother Firth's.

The nation's capital has all but forgotten where this entertainment mecca was located, but if we want to remember that fun is not forgotten in Ottawa, maybe we should find the place that fun began.

Let's go find Mother Firth's.

A Pub Beloved by John By

When Colonel John By first sailed up the Ottawa river in 1826 he was heading toward a settlement called Wrightville on the north shore, named after its founder, American Philemon Wright, who had arrived in 1800.

The south shore of the river, where Ottawa is today, had no settlement and was sparsely settled. As part of his pre-construction survey for the Rideau Canal, By sketched the river, the Chaudiere Islands and much of the south shore.

There weren't a lot of buildings for him to sketch, but one that clearly caught his attention, and that he lovingly rendered in his sketchbook, was a building he called Mrs. Firth's Tavern.

Mother Firth's was opened in 1819 by Mary Dalmahoy, a brazen Scottish woman who soon married Englishman Isaac Firth. Legend has it Isaac followed Dalmahoy to Canada after she turned down his marriage proposal. Second time was the charm.

The tavern soon became indispensable to John By's nascent town. Thirsty travelers, fur traders, voyageurs, raftsmen, military personnel — they all gathered at Mother Firth's for ale, spirits and food. Originally a log cabin structure, the Firth's expanded their tavern operation (with the financial assistance of John By) to include a two-storey hotel, stables and barns to accommodate the town's growing population.

Mother Firth's was a second home to people from all walks of life — decorated military captains drank with mill workers and raftsmen; merchants sang songs with voyageurs. It was a place where stories were told, songs were sung and Ottawa's first identity— tough little lumber town — was born.

The pub was almost closed when John Lebreton purchased the land upon which the tavern sat and then tried to flip it at a 500 per cent mark up to John By. The builder of the Rideau Canal was so offended by the scheme that he changed the route of the proposed canal to make sure none of it would be built upon Lebreton's land.

The Firth's operated their pub until 1832, but future owners of the

↖ Andrew King's sketch recreating the tavern complex.
RIGHT: Isaac Firth, the Englishman whom Mary Dalmahoy married soon after opening Mother Firth's in 1819.

Readers' Remarks

Really a wonderful story. Ottawa's first pub. Wow! — *Larry*

I read about Mrs. Firth's Tavern while researching my book *Capital Walks: Walking Tours of Ottawa* back in 1990 for McLelland and Stewart. In the second edition, I also mentioned Mrs. McGuinty's Tavern that was along the Rideau Canal in what was called "Corkstown." — *Katherine*

Oh, to know what they served! I am a student of whisky. I would have enjoyed tasting what sort of ale, beer, etc. was consumed. — *William*

tavern stopped serving in 1836. The tavern then closed around 1860 and was soon forgotten, as Ottawa's landscape changed and evolved, new development quickly hiding any trace of it.

So where exactly *was* Mother Firth's?

Down a Garden Path

By super-imposing old maps onto modern ones, we can pinpoint the area where this legendary tavern once stood. It would have been located where the Canadian War Museum is today, by the north-east end of the building. The War Museum was opened in 2005, but before construction could begin, an archeological assessment had to be completed. The assessment was done between 2002-2004 by Past Recovery Archeological Services. The report states that a foundation was unearthed and labeled as site BiFW-53. This was Mother Firth's Tavern.

A stage 4 assessment of the Firth Tavern site was completed by Jacques Whitford Environment Ltd. and it was found that:

remnants included a small part of the original, circa 1818–1819 log tavern building, the stone foundation from a late 1830s addition to the second tavern building constructed in the late 1820s, and the southern

Colonel By's map showing Firth's Tavern.

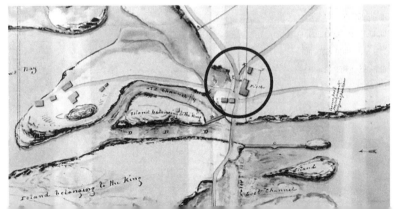

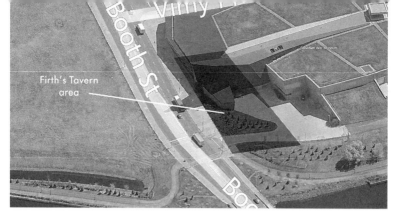

The site of Firth's tavern on the grounds of the Canadian War Museum, indicated by shading.

portion of a stable or shed to the east of the tavern complex constructed in the early 1830s. The artifact assemblage led the researchers to conclude that the tavern had likely ceased operations sometime in the early 1860s.

The assessment concluded by saying "there were no further concerns for the Firth Tavern site" and it was subsequently reburied and built over. No remains or plaque have been erected on the site to indicate the location of Mother Firth's or its importance to Ottawa's history. Today, a garden and concrete path cover the site of Ottawa's first pub.

Using Colonel By's original map and sketch I was able to recreate an image of how Firth's Tavern would have looked during its heyday as Ottawa's first party place. The original log cabin tavern of 1819 and the two-storey hotel addition and stables are as accurately portrayed as my interpretation of the old maps and knowledge of 1820s architecture will allow.

The 2002–2004 archeological assessment in preparation for the building of the Canadian War Museum revealed remains of the tavern's structure.

North Trench

21 THE STONE OF PARLIAMENT

For over a century Canada's parliament buildings have weathered the sands of time, pollution, salt and seismic activity, standing firm as the seat of this country's government. Destroyed by fire in 1916, the original 1859 parliament buildings were rebuilt using Canada's finest building stones of the era.

But where did these stones actually come from? Hidden from view off the 417 Highway there lies a lost quarry, overgrown and forgotten, where Canada's parliament buildings were born.

Nepean Sandstone

The parliament buildings were rebuilt using what was considered Canada's finest building stones — Nepean sandstone. It came, as the name suggests, from the Township of Nepean. Nepean sandstone is a mid-to-late-Cambrian rock found to the west of Ottawa near Bells Corners. Many of us drive over a bed of it on the ridge between Moodie Drive and Kanata.

Nepean s.andstone is a well-cemented sandstone of nearly pure quartz, and it was used not only to build the 1916 parliament buildings, but also the Museum of Nature, the Royal Canadian Mint and the Dominion

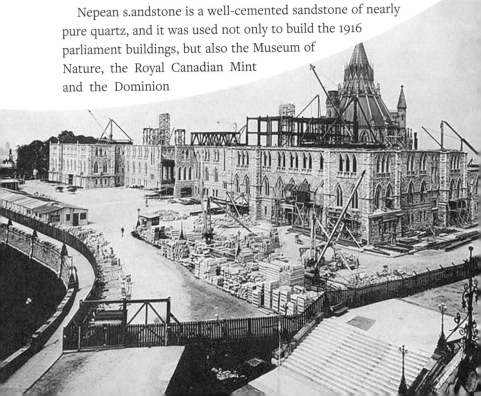

Overlaying the old map on a current map, the quarry can easily be located.

Observatory. Stone from this quarry also provided the blocks needed to build Langevin Building (since renamed the Office of the Prime Minister and the Privy Council) and the old Nepean Town Hall in Westboro.

This quote from the owner of the quarry, who received a shocking order right after the 1916 fire, is from *GeoScience* Canada, Volume 28, Number 1, 2001:

> *Our first order came from Peter Lyall Construction Company for 1,000 tons of sandstone, all for the Parliament Buildings. When we got the parliament job there were several hundred men on the job and they just gobbled up the stone. We couldn't get the stone out fast enough. Stone was hauled up to the building site by teams of horses, struggling along poor roads with six-ton loads. Each team could make but one trip a day.*

Extra quarrymen had to be brought in to fulfill the order, along with stone cutters from Scotland. The quarry continued operations under various owners until 1962, when it was expropriated by the National Capital Commission and soon forgotten.

Readers' Remark

I now live in China and just happened to link to an article that brought me to yours. Fascinating! Having lived in Ottawa for years in the '70s as well as having worked in the Parliament Buildings, I had absolutely no idea of the origins of these magnificent stones. — *David*

I used to work at the CANMET Bells Corners Complex north of Timm Drive. Inside the complex is a quarry that was used by CanmetENERGY to store oil drums and retired research equipment. I wouldn't be surprised if some of the parliamentary stones came from this quarry as well. — *Ted*

Recently I started working in Bells Corners and at lunch I walk on the nearby trails. I noticed the piles of stones that can be seen from the paths and had been wondering what they were. Many ideas crossed my mind, but not a quarry. — *Cathy*

So where exactly did this special stone come from? A 1964 report from the Ontario Department of Mines says that Campbell Quarries is where Canada's parliamentary stone came from, and gives concession and lot numbers for the quarry.

The numbers matched up to an area on an old map of mine marked as "White Sand Quarry." Overlaying this old map with a Google Map of the area shows me where the stones that built parliament would have been located.

The forgotten quarry lies just off an NCC bikepath, and mere metres from Highway 417. With camera in hand, I took to the forest and soon found the overgrown remains of the quarry. I am surprised that there is not an historical plaque or marker signifying the site and its importance to the city.

Single large stones are slowly consumed by the growing forest.

Piles of unused cut stones litter the forest floor, only metres from a bike path.

It is clearly visible where the stonemasons would have worked over a hundred years ago.

A large unused block, never needed for the Parliament Buildings.

MHV SPECTRA 1

22 THE MYSTERY OF THE SPECTRA HOVER VEHICLE

The year was 1970 and south of Ottawa a company was building hovercraft vehicles. Dubbed the Spectra-1, this unique vehicle was straight out of a James Bond film of the same era. The mysterious company that made them also seems a bit Bond-like.

The company was the Modern Hover Vehicles, and it introduced the Spectra in 1970. The hovercraft had an air-cooled, 18.5 hp, single-cylinder hover engine and similar propulsion engine. The orange, fiberglass-bodied hovercraft could travel at speeds of up to 45 mph on land and 40 mph on water, yet over ice the Spectra would reach a blazing 60 mph.

The Modern Hover Vehicles sales brochure touted the Spectra-1 as the "in thing for the in people" and photos show the hovercraft traveling over the rapids of the Ottawa River near the Champlain Bridge.

The company improved on the Spectra-1 design and launched the Spectra-2 in 1973. The Spectra-2 used bigger two-stroke engines and had an enclosed Plexiglas cockpit windshield for the driver.

The Spectra-2 was, according to the Modern Hover Vehicles sales brochure of that year, "The most advanced light hovercraft in the world," and was intended for geological, armed forces, police and rescue use.

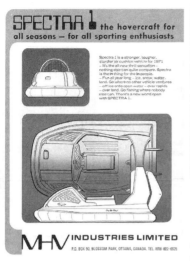

SPECTRA 1 the hovercraft for all seasons — for all sporting enthusiasts

MHV INDUSTRIES LIMITED
P.O. BOX 50, BLOSSOM PARK, OTTAWA, CANADA. TEL (613) 822-6525

LEFT: Sales brochure for the Spectra-1.
ABOVE: The enclosed canopy of the Spectra-2.

Curiously, the company gave its address as 1078 Queensdale Avenue, which according to Goggle Maps does not exist. Nor are there any records I could find telling me what happened to Modern Hover Vehicles. A fellow on Twitter said he had acquired a Spectra-1 (see photo) and is in the process of restoring it, but that is the only one I have ever seen.

It is currently not known what happened to the mysterious Ottawa-born Spectra hovercraft, the company that made them, or if any other vehicles are still in existence.

↖ The Spectra-1, made in Ottawa, in a photo from the 1971 sales brochure of it on the Ottawa River. Note the Champlain Bridge in the background.
RIGHT: A Spectra-1 in the United States awaiting restoration by owner Matt Norman.

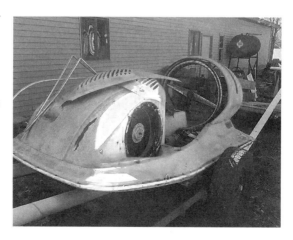

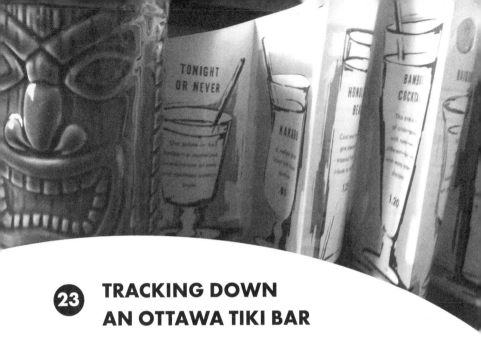

23 TRACKING DOWN AN OTTAWA TIKI BAR

Every city has its favourite nightclubs, and every decade has its hot spots. In the 1960s, one of the hottest, or should I say coolest nightclubs in Ottawa was the Beachcomber Room.

The Beachcomber was located in the Talisman Motor Inn on Carling Avenue, and boasted the latest in tiki culture and entertainment. The Talisman was designed by the man who founded Kanata, William Teron. (The similarities end there.)

Built in 1963 as Ottawa's premier business convention centre and hotel, Teron designed the Talisman with a South Pacific theme, including a very faithful replica of a tranquil Japanese garden at the center of the motel. The Beachcomber Room was flamboyantly decorated in a Tahitian motif that featured a 90-foot mural painted by Count Alex van Svodoba, who also painted murals at Carleton University.

The Polynesian theme of the Beachcomber Room was in tune with the popularity of tiki culture during the mid-century era, which was based primarily on Don the Beachcomber in Hollywood, California. Credited with being the first tiki restaurant in North America, its founder, Donn Beach, was the first to mix flavored syrups and fresh fruit juices with rum.

Original 1960s postcard of the Talisman Motor Inn that contained the Beachcomber Room.

His restaurant became the hot ticket for Hollywood stars, making the tiki theme a North American phenomenon. Ottawa was no exception, with The Tabu opening in the old Beacon Arms Hotel (now the Capital Hotel & Suites) in the early-'60s and The Beachcomber Room opening soon afterwards in 1963, taking its name directly from the original Hollywood establishment.

The original Japanese garden.

Readers' Remarks

Local jazz pianist Brian Browne
used to be part of The Beachcomber's
house band and once regaled me
with tales of the shenanigans that used
to go on there. Who knew Ottawa
had such a wild side? — *Joanna*

As a young musician I played
in the band on New Years Eve of
1997 at the Beachcomber. The room
had just reopened for the first time
in years and was being used for
mystery theatre dinners, which were
popular at that time. Even though
I was too young to appreciate the
mid-century era, I was pretty taken
at how the Tiki Bar was completely
intact. A total time capsule! — *Phil*

Thanks for running this, Andrew.
Brought back many memories of
going dancing there is the mid-
'70s to very early '80s. — *Robert*

I bartended there from
1979 to its sad closing on
January 1, 1991. — *Denis*

**WOW, that brings back
good memories** of hearing
The Platters perform there in 1974.
Amazing atmosphere! Thanks for
writing about The Talisman and the
Beachcomber Room. — *Chris*

Spent many fun times in the Tiki
Room. Married my first husband
in 1967 in the Japanese garden as
people watched from their balcony
rooms. The manager was Ross
Sansom and the maitre d' in the
dining room made a terrific Caesar
salad as well as Spanish coffee right
at your table. Great memories. — *Lee*

The Beachcomber Room soon became the place to dance, listen to live music and enjoy the quintessential Tiki Mai Tai cocktail. It stayed that way for nearly three decades. However, as with most bars, its popularity eventually waned and the Talisman name was dropped when it became a Travelodge. The hotel was extensively renovated, with the Japanese pond turned into a kid's water park and the Polynesian theme was dumped.

Remnants of the Japanese gardens are still visible today, though, as are some architectural details from its illustrious past. These photos show all that is left of Ottawa's fabled Beachcomber Room.

Japanese garden today.

The unique 1960s architectural style by Bill Teron is still evident.

Some relics from the old Polynesian-themed Talisman can be spotted around the present day hotel.

Another relic, a Japanse hutch.

THE LOST VILLAGE OF LONG ISLAND

24

Just south of Ottawa, before you reach the town of Manotick on River Road, there is a popular Rideau Canal lock station called Long Island Locks. Surrounded by quiet, empty fields of gently swaying long grass, there is a crumbling ruin of an old farmhouse. This lone old house was not always in such solitude, but was once surrounded by a bustling village called Long Island.

No trace of this multi-block town can be found today, but streets, a church, hotels and a post office were all part of this community back in the mid-19th century. Where did it go and why did it vanish without a trace? Let's explore the area of this once-thriving community that seems to have vanished from time and space.

Ghostly Past

First settled in the 1830s during the construction of the Rideau Canal, the village of Long Island seems to be shrouded in obscurity, its exact location difficult to pinpoint. At its peak, in the mid-1860s, the village contained general stores, two churches and its own post office. However, once Moss Kent Dickinson built a stately stone flourmill and established the nearby village of Manotick, many of the original settlers moved there and the village of Long Island went into decline.

Not much evidence of its existence seems to have survived, just a few sketches and the map of the village as drawn for the County

The village of Long Island and the locks depicted in 19th-century paintngs.

Atlas of 1880. So, using that map and overlaying that with current Google Maps, we can pinpoint with accuracy where this ghost village was actually situated.

The village must have gone into decline in the early part of the 20th century, as it seems to have disappeared from maps after that time. Was there a sweeping fire that tragically reduced the village to ash? Did the government expropriate the village and bulldoze it out of history?

Once we overlay the 1880 map onto a current map we can see exactly the location of the ghost village, and many features of the boundaries match up with the current terrain. In order to investigate it properly, though, an on-site wander was necessary.

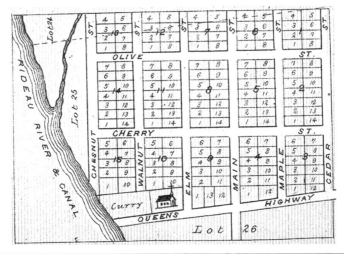

19th-century map of the village of Long Island, then the same map superimposed on a contemporary aerial view

If you blinked you'd miss it if you were driving down River Road, as years of overgrowth have obscured most of the original site, yet one key element remains: a deserted graveyard. Toppled tombstones and stone obelisks dot the landscape at the site of what was once the churchyard, as sketched on the original map.

The church seems to have long since been removed, but its interred parishioners still remain, a ghostly reminder of the village long gone. A wander through and examination of the toppled stone markers shows dates in the 1880s, probably when the church was still functioning, but I could not see any dates after that so I am assuming the church yard was not used after the 1890s.

A further wander into the area revealed no trace of the village, only the creek that is mapped out on the original map. A trek to the shore of the river reveals many bricks strewn around as if the town was bulldozed into the river. I would imagine an archeological dig could unearth many fragments of evidence that prove the village was once there, but alas, I do not have that access and leave it up to the proper authorities to investigate this ghost village further.

It is fascinating to know that a vibrant, thriving village once existed where nothing exists today, other than swaying grass and picnicking boaters. I recommend you check it out yourself one day, and take a walk through the Lost Village of Long Island.

A trek to the shore of the river reveals many bricks strewn around as if the town was bulldozed into the river.

Readers' Remarks

It is sad to see abandoned and derelict gravestones. If nothing else, it would be nice to find records of those buried there and commemorate their remains somehow. — *Dianne*

For your next adventure, check the Village of Fallowfield. — *Bill*

Thanks for the story. I spent a good number of summers at the Long Island RCMP camp in the 1950s. Don't recall anyone mentioning the vanished town. My father was usually up on that type of history, but guess he didn't know about it. — *Jim*

Hello. I currently live in the original Long Island village. I am in lot 25, section 4, units 5,6,7 and 8 on what would have been Main Street and Cherry Street. I am excited to have just learned of your website. — *Earl*

We moved to a house on Long Island in Manotick back in 2010 and I've really enjoyed researching the history of the area. There are some old books with mention of the Long Island village in the Manotick Public Library — seems like the people in the original village just shifted to cluster around the Manotick mill when it was built around 1860. — *Danielle*

25 SOLSTICE SECRETS

Being the nation's capital, Ottawa is filled with many curious structures, from incredible museums to stunning historical architecture that fills the downtown core. Yet there are other intriguing structures that go unnoticed unless a more detailed and closer inspection is made, structures that are mysterious in nature and without clear explanation.

Once such structure is a bizarre concrete pad in Ottawa's scenic Major's Hill Park. I've walked over it many times, but didn't realize until recently the oddity of the whole thing. A glimpse at it from an aerial image illustrates its very esoteric nature.

It seems to be a carefully crafted solstice monument, one that interprets an event that has been celebrated among many ancient cultures with various rituals and themes of religion or fertility.

But why is there an unmarked solstice structure in downtown Ottawa?

The Mystery of Major's Hill Park

I have previously investigated another odd solstice site in Ottawa, at the former city hall on Green Island. The pyramids built into the roofline of that building, designed by architect Moshe Safdie, mysteriously align with the solstice.

Now another site has been found, this one in Major's Hill Park, across from Parliament Hill. The park is owned and maintained by the National Capital Commission, which boasts that Major's Hill Park is the capital's first park and has been a green space since 1826, when the building of the Rideau Canal began. In 1867, fireworks and bonfires at Major's Hill Park marked our first Canada Day celebrations.

The park was once occupied by labourers working on the nearby Rideau Canal, and more notably it was the official residence of Lieutenant-Colonel John By until he returned to England in 1832. Once referred to as Colonel's Hill, Captain Daniel Bolton replaced Colonel By and moved into his old house. Bolton was later promoted to Major and since then the area has been called Major's Hill. The ruins of the original stone house were later unearthed and are part of the park today.

After researching the odd elliptical concrete pad at the south end of the park to determine why it was built in such an intriguing manner, I found nothing about who designed or built it. I turned to aerial imagery, to see if an answer might be found there. Sure enough, it has a very specific alignment. Applying the Sun Surveyor app to the site, it was revealed that the structure is part of some bizarre summer solstice monument that spreads across the park.

The oval shaped concrete pad is divided into emanating lines from a marked circle with a distinct black line with dashed white lines that points to the north west. If you stand in the centre of the circle and look down that black line, your sightline carries across the park to a

The concrete pad has a circle with divisional lines and a single dark line pointing to the northwest.

SECONDARY "SOLSTICE RUNWAY"

sightline of setting sun
on summer solstice

PRIMARY SOLSTICE CENTRE   viewpoint

Diagram showing the alignment of the primary and secondary runways with the setting of the sun on summer solstice.

The view looking back towards the primary oval from the secondary solstice runway. Note the ruins of Colonel By's home to the left of the end of the runway strip.

secondary concrete structure that also contains an odd runway that resembles an airport landing strip. This secondary runway area intersects with the stone ruins of Colonel By's original home.

Once the summer solstice date of June 21 has been entered into the app we can see that the whole structure is in alignment with the setting sun. What this means is that if you are standing in the centre of the circle on the primary concrete pad looking down the black line as the sun sets on the summer solstice, you would see the sun disap-pear in perfect alignment with the concrete "runway" that stretches across the park.

Wait — There's More

What is really fascinating is that if you extend that sightline even further, past the secondary runway, it perfectly intersects with another curious Ottawa structure: The statue of Samuel de Champlain at Nepean Point.

One alignment match could be coincidence, two is unlikely, but three? I still don't know what to make of that third alignment, but if you want to have some fun with it, consider this: Samuel de Champlain may have been a Knight Templar.

There is so little verified personal information about Champlain (we don't even know what he looked like) that everything about the man should be taken with a grain of salt, but according to the 1890 book *History of the Knights Templar of Canada*, compiled by historians of the Order, Champlain was the first Knight to reach the New World.

Whatever you think of the claim, it is interesting to note that Champlain had an estate in La Rochelle, where the Knights Templar had a strong presence. La Rochelle was where the Knights stationed their main fleet of ships. It was also the port from which Champlain set out for many of his voyages to North America.

Could it be true? Well, here's one more fun fact to ponder. The Champlain statue — sculpted by Hamilton McCarthy and erected in 1915 — famously placed Champlain's astrolabe upside down in his outreached hand. Why is the inaccurate astrolabe so prominently displayed, and in perfect alignment with the sun on the day of the summer solstice?

Readers' Remarks

What an amazing feature at Major's Hill – never knew – will definitely look closer at it next time I'm downtown. Great research. — *Katherine*

I have just come across this post and I am intrigued. Being a bit sceptical, I drew my own line across a Google map and certainly verified the alignment. So it's on my calendar to revisit at midsummer evening. — *Murray*

Thanks to your marvelous post, the jig's up and soon you will have ersatz Druids chanting all over it every year. — *Urspo*

I think the pad is actually an unfinished sundial built in the mid-90s by Malette Granite for the NCC. The company went bankrupt midway through the project. They were also responsible for the three little monuments sitting around the sundial with plaques and the chimney type thing at the other end of the park. I can't explain Champlain. — *Pierre*

Well, if you take a closer look at the astrolabe, you will see a shape that curiously resembles the cross of the Knights Templar. The summer solstice, by the way, was revered by the Knights Templar, one of their holiest days, one set aside for solemn ceremony and ritual.

This is all fun speculation, but it is curious how two mysterious solstice monuments in Major's Hill Park line up perfectly with what can easily be seen as a Templar cross, held aloft on the tallest point of land along the river. Whatever does it all mean?

The statue of Samuel de Champlain at Nepean Point. On the Summer Solstice, an alignment with the sun, the astrolabe, the runway and the viewing platform occurs, as shown in the diagram below.

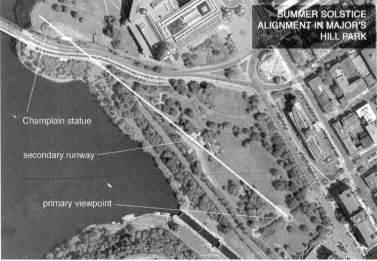

SUMMER SOLSTICE ALIGNMENT IN MAJOR'S HILL PARK

Champlain statue

secondary runway

primary viewpoint

The Lost Lighthouses of the Ottawa River

Along the Ottawa River, a few hundred metres north of Beacon Hill, can be found the remains of a lost lighthouse. Constructed in 1860 between the gaps of the Ducks Islands near the provincial border, the lighthouse was built as a navigational aid to warn sailors of the dangerous reef known as "Green Shoal."

Navigating ships on the Ottawa River was a relatively new adventure when the lighthouse was built. There hadn't been a need for much more than canoes until the completion of the Rideau Canal in 1832 and the Carillon Canal in 1833. Soon the Ottawa River became a busy transportation route connecting Ottawa and Montreal in the days before full train service.

The large number of shoals and islands east of Ottawa created hazards, though, for the steamships that had arrived. There was soon an urgent need for lighthouses and warning beacons. The government of the day ordered the construction of approximately 30 lighthouses along the Ottawa River.

Pre-Confederation Canadian lighthouses were usually built of stone or brick, but with the need to build so many structures, so quickly, the newly formed Department of Marine and Fisheries required cheaper and faster lighthouse construction techniques.

Built as four-sided, tapered wooden clapboard towers, these structures had the advantage of being inexpensive to build and, in some cases, could be relocated if needed. They are typical of the lighthouse beacons built along the Ottawa River.

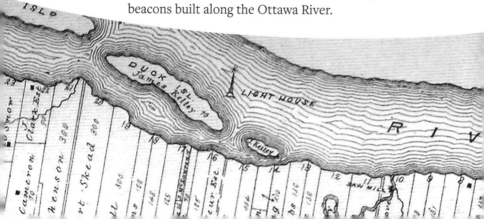

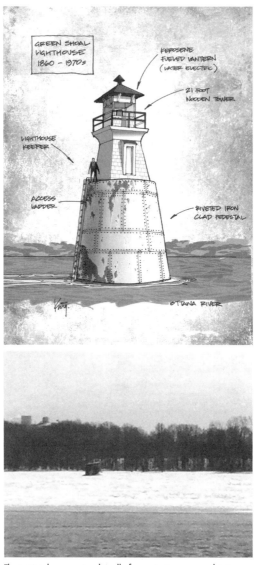

The rusting beacon ruins, literally frozen in time, encased in ice on the Ottawa Rivr. The neighbourhood of Beacon Hill, which got its name from this very lighthouse, is in the background.

Green Shoal would see the construction of its beacon in 1860 on a conical pedestal sheathed in iron boiler plates, riveted together like some kind of Jules Verne rocket to withstand the strong river current and sheets of crushing ice carried downstream.

Atop this iron clad pedestal was placed a four-sided, white wooden pyramidal tower 21 feet in height. Using a standard design used for many of the Ottawa River lighthouses, the structure housed a fixed light that was initially fueled by kerosene, a fuel invented by the Canadian geologist Abraham Gesner in 1846.

The Green Shoal lighthouse was visible to passing ships from a distance of nine miles and was rebuilt in 1900, when it was most likely converted to electricity.

In 1862, the Sessional Papers of the Province of Canada show a house was requested for the keeper of the Green Shoals lighthouse, yet its location or fate is unknown today. In 1891, lighthouse keeper A. Laberge earned an annual salary of $250 for his duties maintaining the lighthouse at Green Shoal.

The lighthouse remained in operation for more than 100 years, finally being dismantled and replaced by an automated beacon in the 1970s. It was at this time that a new suburb was being developed nearby. The old beacon on the river below was visible from atop the hill on what is now Naskapi Drive, and thus the neighbourhood got its name.

Today Beacon Hill residents and those on the Quebec side of the river can still see the ironclad lighthouse ruins sitting in the Ottawa River. Bashed by years of crushing river ice, the rusty remnants now list to one side, a forgotten sentinel literally frozen in time during the winter months.

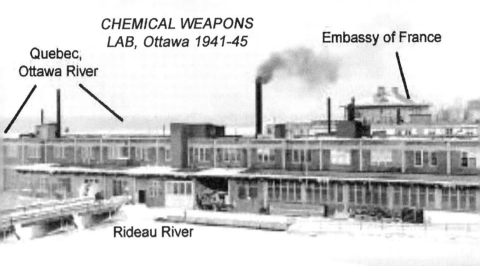

CHEMICAL WEAPONS
LAB, Ottawa 1941–45

Embassy of France

Quebec,
Ottawa River

Rideau River

27 THE SECRET CHEMICAL WEAPONS LAB AT RIDEAU FALLS

Being the nation's capital, Ottawa has always been home to top-secret, classified projects. These projects are developed in utter secrecy, details about them not being revealed until years later, if at all. A scenic park beside Rideau Falls may seem an unlikely spot for one of these projects.

But it was, and not just any classified project. This one was about as top-secret as it gets: a laboratory, built inside an old pulp and paper mill, for the development and testing of chemical weapons.

Chemical Weapons and Ottawa: A Brief History

Allied forces during World War II made preparations to wage both chemical and biological warfare. The use of chemical and biological weapons had already been experienced in World War I, with ghastly results. The threat of bio/chem weapons being used again was supposed to have been removed with the signing of the 1925 Geneva Protocol, a treaty prohibiting the use of chemical and biological weapons in international armed conflicts.

↑ The chemical weapons lab at Rideau Falls, in a building that was once a pulp and paper mill.

Yet here in Ottawa, there was not only manufacturing of chemical weapons during World War II, there was also human experimentation.

The year was 1941 and the National Research Council (NRC) was part of a program to study the use of choking gases such as chlorine and chloropicrin, in addition to hellish compounds like hydrogen cyanide and cyanogen chloride. Ottawa's studies also included blistering weapons such as the infamous mustard gas. It may seem hard to believe today, but labs in Canada studied, tested, manufactured and stockpiled these bio/chem weapons during World War II.

Research was headed by the Directorate of Chemical Warfare and Smoke and conducted in Canadian university labs using NRC grant programs. These school labs included McGill, Toronto, Queen's and Western. Ottawa had its own chemical weapons laboratory in a now-demolished NRC facility by the Rideau Falls.

Created in 1940, the Rideau Falls chemical weapons lab, dubbed CWL, was responsible for the production of flame-thrower fuel and the manufacture of 1,000 pounds of B1 dye used to detect mustard gas. By the end of the war, CWL had also produced 8 million gas masks, 40 million canisters, and in Cornwall, produced barrels of deadly mustard gas.

The Ottawa labs worked on highly toxic but largely unknown chemical agents. Once a converted pulp and paper mill known as

Current view of what used to be the chemical weapons lab.

Edward Mills, the secret lab operated from 1940 until 1947, when operations were transferred to a site at Shirley's Bay. The labs were demolished soon after the move-out and the site eventually became Rideau Falls Park.

As part of the study, testing and manufacture of bio/chem weapons, the CWL labs at Rideau Falls also conducted experiments on humans. Paid volunteers would be subjected to testing of chemical agents, with experimental counter measures being tested for their success. Subjects suffered blisters, and respiratory testing. In February 2004, the Ministers of National Defence and Veterans Affairs announced a program to recognize and compensate Canadian veterans who had volunteered to participate in chemical-warfare experiments conducted in Ottawa.

After World War II, the stockpiled chemical and biological weapons were taken aboard ships and unceremoniously dumped into the Atlantic Ocean, where barrel upon barrel of these nightmarish compounds decay on the ocean floor.

Photos of the manufacturing of chemical and biological weapons at the Rideau Falls labs.

When Glen Gower from *OttawaStart* told me a story about a hiker who stumbled across the remains of an old motel playground in the NCC Greenbelt I was interested in teaming up on an expedition to find it.

Doing some preliminary research on the possibility of there being a lost motel in the woods of the Greenbelt, I referred to a 1965 aerial image of the area to see what was there. Sure enough, not one, but two motels can clearly be seen in the aerial image.

Taking those images and overlaying them on a current aerial image provided a bearing on the approximate locations. I then started some historical research. What were these places? What happened to them?

A quick search of what motels could have been in the area showed that the stretch of road they were on was called Whiskey Road in the mid-1800s. This was because there were so many taverns in the vicinity, as this was a midway point between Ottawa and Richmond while travelling on the Richmond Road. Now part of Robertson Road in Bells Corners, the road was also once known as Old Highway 15 and 7 during the mid-20th century.

It was a stretch of road that was a continuation of both Highway 7 and Highway 15 and it was the only corridor into Ottawa from the west. Being so, a number of motels began to spring up along this road, most notably during the '50s when "motoring" was a popular tourist activity and "motor hotels," or "motels" as they were soon called, became a popular option for weary drivers and their passengers.

An Internet search soon gave me the names of the two motels that would have been in today's Greenbelt: Charlie's Motel, and slightly to the east of

↺ Charlie's Motel from a 1950s postcard. ABOVE, a 1965 aerial view showing the striped roof.

that, the Cedarview Motel. I located 1950s postcards of both motels. The bizarre diagonal roof striping shown on a 1965 aerial photo confirmed that structure must have been Charlie's Motel.

With both motels now identified, further research showed that they were later purchased by the National Capital Commission. An *Ottawa Citizen* article from 1965 states the NCC bought Charlie's that year and was leasing it back to proprietor Howard Soucie for a three-year contract. A 1976 aerial image shows both motels were still standing at that time, but a 1979 *Ottawa Journal* article and photo shows that the Cedarview burned down that year. It is not known when or how Charlie's Motel disappeared.

A Walk in the Woods

Overlaying the known locations with a current map, Glen and I were able to locate where the remains of these mid-century motels should lie. Arranging to meet nearby, we happened to pick one of the coldest days of the winter for our expedition, and needless to say, a half hour into our adventure our cameras and batteries began to freeze. Keeping them close to our bodies for restorative warmth, we trudged through the -20°C temperatures and crunching snow to discover the site of Charlie's Motel.

Nothing much is left of Charlie's; just an empty field with some surrounding trees. Perhaps in the summer, more of the ruins are visible, but on our trek we decided to keep moving through the NCC Greenbelt woodlands towards whatever remained of the Cedarview Motel.

The Cedarview Motel from a 1950s postcard, and a 1965 aerial image. Note the swimming pool.

Making our way through the snow covered trees, we came across the area where the Cedarview would have been. The whole area is actually full of cedar trees, so the hotel had been aptly named 60 years ago.

The 1965 aerial image of the Cedarview showed that it once had an in-ground swimming pool, a feature filled in as shown on the 1976 image. Stumbling through the deep snow, we soon came across a clearing with absolutely no vegetation growing on it. Was this the filled-in swimming pool? Overgrowth had consumed the Cedarview Motel area, but for some reason, this area was devoid of any trees, which I think would be because the trees would not be able to take root within an in-ground concrete swimming pool.

Part of the foundation of the Cedarview Motel.

The concrete foundation of the Cedarview is clearly lying among the overgrown forest of cedars. The long, straight shape of the motel rooms illustrated on the aerial image and on the postcard were discovered buried under the snow, running through the forest of trees that reclaimed the footprint of the original motel. The outline of the motel structure lay hidden in the forest, slowly being enveloped by the cedar forest from which it was named, the only remnants of its fiery demise.

Other motel artifacts were discovered as Glen and I searched the area, including concrete forms, barrier posts, more foundations, wooden fence posts and piles of rubble. The majority of the Cedarview Motel lies hidden beneath the forest canopy of cedar trees for which it was named, a hidden reminder of its past accommodating weary motorists on their way to or from the Nation's Capital.

The ruins of the Cedarview Motel and Charlie's Motel sit silently in the woods of the Greenbelt, a by-product of the NCC's vision of a green space for the city and its tourists to enjoy. But evidently, with no vacancy on Robertson Road.

Nepean fire department arrived after the Cedarview Motel was already ablaze.

The Wreck of the *Jean Richard* 29

I am fascinated by maps. After scanning an aerial photo of downtown Ottawa one day, I noticed what appeared to be the outline of a ship's hull along the shore of the Ottawa River.

With the Ottawa River being a major supply route for hundreds of years, I've heard of many shipwrecks lying below the river's surface. Aerial maps can be deceptive, but this clearly looked like a ship half submerged in the water. I decided to go see what was there.

I found the wreck without any difficulty (exactly where my map said it would be). I sketched and measured the ship's hull shape and filmed what was there, then headed back to the city.

What, exactly, had I found?

Looking for Clues

After scouring the Internet and libraries, but finding nothing about my mysterious shipwreck, I contacted my good friend Glen at OttawaStart. Always one to help out and promote local history, Glen spread the word about my discovery through his popular website, asking for any information.

The *Ottawa Citizen* and *CBC News* caught wind of the story and proceeded to do their own research, even calling in a representative from the Eastern Ontario chapter of "Save Our Ships" to help solve the riddle. But the shipwreck I had found remained a mystery.

Clips from the NFB film about the building of the *Jean-Richard*.

I continued on my own, scouring nautical books, trying to access the archives of the Great Lakes Maritime Museum, but I soon reached the same dead end the *Citizen* and CBC had reached.

Then, four months after I first contacted him, Glen sent me a Twitter message with an old map attached. The map had been made by the Underwater Society of Ottawa and showed various shipwrecks in the Ottawa River. The wreck I had found was clearly shown on the map.

That wasn't all. The map also gave the shipwreck a name —the *Jean Richard*.

The Pride of Petite-Rivière Saint-François

It turned out the *Jean Richard* had quite an interesting past, and a rather special place in Canadian history.

The ship was built in 1959 at Petite-Rivière Saint-François, a small village about 100 km upriver from Quebec City. The shipbuilders are listed as master carpenters Philippe Lavoie and Paul-Émile Carré. Knowing that the days of wooden ships on the St. Lawrence River were coming to an end, the National Film Board (NFB) sent a crew

The *Jean-Richard*, just about to be launched.

to record the building of the *Jean Richard*.

The film was shot by Ottawa's own Crawley Films, and the NFB's timing was rather good as the *Jean Richard* would be the last wooden schooner built at Petite-Rivière, a shipbuilding village that had launched wooden ships onto the St. Lawrence River for more than two centuries.

I quickly contacted the NFB and they courteously couriered the film to me, which I immediately watched, studied and compared to my Ottawa shipwreck photos. The 96-foot long, 28-foot wide *Jean Richard* shown in the NFB film was indeed a match with my shipwreck.

The 30-minute film ended with an all-night party and then the Jean Richard was launched at dawn on May 23, 1959. So how did the last wooden schooner built on the St. Lawrence River end up as a shipwreck on a quiet bay in the Ottawa River?

Readers' Remarks

My father worked to build the Jean-Richard. It was built about one mile from my house! He told me the name of the men in the pictures! He feels bad when I show him these pictures. He is 85 years now. — *Roger*

About 50 years ago, my buddy and I had just finished scuba diving and were walking up the beach in Constance Bay. The local handyman, Len Purcell, (the road to our community center was named after him) passed us and asked if we were looking for the alligator. We laughed and said we were too busy looking for crocodiles. "No, no," he said, "it was sunk right out there," as his arm swung in an arc. We ignored him and put away our stuff. ... Fast-forward 40 years to the Quality Inn restaurant in Arnprior. I walked in and saw a mural depicting loggers on a log boom with a strange boat. The bottom of the picture said "Alligator." I was stunned. I now believe one is sunk off the end of Len Purcell Drive. — *Gerry*

It's amazing that this historic boat has been able to "sit there" in the water for over 25 years. Great story, Andrew. — *Glen*

On the St. Lawrence River sometime in the 1960s.

Thirty Years of Service

After it was launched, the *Jean Richard* worked for almost twenty years on the St. Lawrence River, before being brought up the Ottawa River and converted into a "disco cruise ship" and renamed the *Ville de Vanier*.

Operating out of the Hull Marina for many years starting in 1976, the ship was later converted into a floating cottage. It is believed a fire scorched the wooden ship in 1987 and the charred remains were hauled off and abandoned in the concealed inlet where I found it.

This once glorious ship was the last of its kind, a ship grand enough to be documented by the National Film Board, one of great nautical importance to our region, but now left to decay in eight feet of water, not five minutes from downtown Ottawa.

The *Jean Richard* should be saved and preserved for future generations, much like the NFB did when they filmed it being built sixty years ago. In this particular case, we can truthfully say that the likes of the *Jean Richard* will never be seen again.

Renamed *Ville de Vanier* in 1976 when it became an Ottawa River cruise ship.

THE PARLIAMENT BUILDINGS AND THE KNIGHTS TEMPLAR

30

Ottawa contains some of the most stunning architecture in the country, with the Parliament Buildings being at the top of the list. They were designed by architect Thomas Fuller, who designed many other prominent buildings in Ottawa, including the formerly named Langevin Block on Parliament Hill and All Saints Church in Westboro.

In studying Fuller's work, I noticed recurring themes and motifs. After a while, these design elements became too obvious to ignore. A bit of historical sleuthing was required.

I needed to find an answer to this question: Was Thomas Fuller, Canada's most prominent architect of the late-19th century, a Knights Templar?

The Order of Knights Templar

Formed in 1120, the Knights Templar was created to protect pilgrims to the Holy Land of Jerusalem. It began with nine knights, but quickly grew under the patronage of the king of France and the pope of the time. The knights built their domed headquarters on what was supposedly the ruins of King Solomon's temple in Jerusalem, hence their name — the Knights of the Temple or "Knights Templar."

A Templar Knight with disctinctive red cross on tunic.

Knights Templar being burned at the stake on Friday, October 13, 1307.

Templar Knights, in their distinctive white cloaks with a red cross, were among the most skilled fighting units of the Crusades. While some fought, other Templars created an economic infrastructure for the Crusades — an early form of banking. They also built castles, fortifications and churches across the Holy Land.

When the Crusades ended and the Holy Land they had been sworn to protect was lost, the Knights Templar were blamed for the defeat by the French court and the Catholic Church, the two institutions that had helped create the Order. On Friday the thirteenth of October 1307 many Knights Templar were rounded up and executed under orders of both King Philip IV of France and Pope Clement. This is one reason why Friday the thirteenth is regarded as an unlucky day.

The Knights Templars who escaped the purge went into hiding throughout Europe, with many making their way to Scotland, where Robert the Bruce gave them sanctuary. (Robert had been ex-communicated by the Pope the year before the Templars purge.) The Knights' skills in masonry, architecture and design can be seen in various churches throughout Scotland and England to this day.

After almost 500 years of hiding from the Catholic Church, the Order of the Knights Templar was resurrected in 1790 by Alexander Deuchar in Scotland under a new name: Freemasonry. Since at least the 18th century, Freemasons have used Templar symbols and rituals. The Freemasons also have five separated degrees or Orders: The Entered Apprentice, The Fellowcraft, The Master Mason, The Royal Arch, and finally, Knights Templar.

Thomas Fuller.

Thomas Fuller and the Knights Templar

Thomas Fuller was born in England and came to Canada in 1857 to set up an architecture firm specializing in stone buildings. Two years later he became Canada's most important architect when he was given the commission to build the Parliament Buildings.

One has to wonder about his quick success. After being awarded the contract to build the Parliament Buildings he went on, in very quick succession, to get commissions for the Langevin Block, St. Albans Church in Ottawa, St. James Church in Perth and many others.

One possible explanation for Fuller's meteoric rise is a story as old as Ottawa — connections. Fuller may have had them through the Order of Freemasons.

The ceremony for laying the cornerstone for the Parliament Buildings was filled with Masonic references and rituals. Sir John A. Macdonald was a well-known Freemason, as were many other parliamentarians of the day. It is easy to imagine these men wanting a Freemason architect to design the country's first federal institutions.

It is also easy to imagine, by looking at the work of Thomas Fuller, that they found one.

The Parliamentary Library

The Parliament Buildings designed by Fuller were destroyed by fire in 1916, the only building to survive being the Library of Parliament. The library was opened on February 28, 1876, and its similarities to Templar churches of medieval times seem too obvious to be a coincidence.

Consider the ceremony as well. On September 1, 1860, the Prince of Wales, Albert Edward, presided over the laying of the cornerstone of the Parliament Buildings. The ceremony included the Prince of Wales and Fuller exchanging Masonic vows while the

The Prince of Wales, Albert Edward, here seen in full Freemason attire.

Comparison of Templar-built structures throughout the ages, with Fuller's Library of Parliament, inset.

Every window of the library is emblazoned with the symbol of the four-petal rose.

stone was lowered. In 1875, Albert Edward became Grand Master of the Convent General of the Knights Templar.

Consider also the design. The rose is an important symbol to both Freemasons and Templar Knights, and there is a rose carved into every window of the Parliamentary Library. Not any rose either, but a four-petal rose, which is synonymous with the Knights Templar, who always looked for balance, also the reason why the Templar Cross is a cross of four equal lengths.

That cross can be found between the petals of every rose found in the Library of Parliament.

St. Albans, St. Paul's and Westboro Churches

Fuller designed these churches within a few years of each other, all in his signature style, one that pays homage to English medieval

The Eye of Parliament

The Eye of Providence, or the All-Seeing Eye of God, is often associated with Freemasonry. It is probably best known for being on the Great Seal of the United States, as depicted on the American one-dollar bill.

The design committee that came up with the idea of using the Eye of Providence on the Great Seal included Benjamin Franklin, a well-known Freemason. The American depiction of the All-Seeing Eye in a triangular shape above an unfinished pyramid was adopted as part of the symbolism on the reverse side of the Great Seal in 1782.

The following decade the Eye of Providence first appeared in Freemason literature in a book by Thomas Smith Webb, *Freemasons Monitor*.

Fast-Forward seventy years and Thomas Fuller is designing Canada's first Parliament Buildings. All that is left of those original Parliament Buildings is the library, after the disastrous fire of 1916.

Is it possible Fuller put Freemason motifs and architectural design elements not just into the library, but all the buildings of Parliament? We can only theorize, but see how easily the Eye of Providence can be superimposed over Canada's original Centre Tower.

Superimposing the Eye of Providence over the original tower and clock we see that the "eye" aligns perfectly with the original round clock. The triangle is also a perfect match in all respects to angles and proportions.

churches and castles. Medieval castle features such as arrow slits were implemented in his church designs as tall, thin windows. Low rooflines and buttressed sidewalls were used in all his designs. The churches also contain many rose motifs.

Fuller went on, after this church-building phase, to become Canada's Chief Dominion Architect. He held this position from 1881 to 1896 and oversaw the construction of more than 150 buildings nationwide. Of these, approximately 78 were federal buildings and post offices, many of which are still standing today.

Could the "IHS" stand for the Freemasonry motto: In Hoc Signo"?

The Final Clue

After studying the architecture of Fuller, I started wondering if there might be a last clue at his final resting place. Thomas Fuller died in 1898 and is interred at Beechwood Cemetery in Ottawa.

With the help of cemetery staff who provided me with historical records and a map, I located where Fuller was buried. If Fuller was indeed a Freemason — perhaps even one with the exalted rank of Knights Templar — his burial site should reflect this.

Trudging through the snow I finally came upon his grave and, sure enough, there above his name was the Templar cross. There was also a strange symbol in the cross, one that, when I sketched it out, looked like the letters IHS, which stands for "Jesus" in Christian symbology.

IHS also means something to Knights Templar. According to the Grand Lodge of Freemasonry Symbology website, IHS stands for "In Hoc Signo," or translated, "By this sign you shall conquer" — the rallying cry, or motto, if you will, of the Knights Templar.

The architect of Canada's Parliament Buildings is buried beneath a Templar cross with the Templar motto. And conquer he certainly did. There are about 140 Fuller-designed buildings left standing across the country: courthouses, post offices and customs offices, found in small towns and large cities.

Next time you happen to see a stately old federal building in your travels, look for the roses and the four-equal-sided crosses, and see if you're looking at a Thomas Fuller masterpiece — a piece of our history inspired by the ancient Order of Knights Templar.

OTTAWA'S LOST MOTELS

31

Being a capital city means Ottawa is a tourist destination, as any visit to the Parliament Buildings will quickly tell you. Out-of-town visitors have been coming to our city to see the sights for more than one-hundred-and-fifty years.

This constant stream of tourists is one of the reasons Ottawa had a "motel boom" in the 1950s and '60s. (The word "motel" didn't enter the dictionary until the 1940s when *Webster's* defined it as a "hotel consisting of a single building of connected rooms whose doors face a parking lot." So we were pretty quick to embrace this new form of visitor accommotation.)

Motels were probably most popular in the '60s, with many being driven out of business soon afterwards when major freeways were built that rerouted tourists away from what had once been popular routes into the city.

Many of the motels that survived have been horribly transformed into grotesque skeletons of their former selves. But there are clues in the architecture about what they once were. Let's go back in time and find some of these cool, lost motels.

Motel de Ville

Located at 333 Montreal Road, this amazing original motel once boasted "radios and televisions" in each room, as well as air conditioning and "large ceramic-tiled bathrooms."

↻ The classic mid-century modern design of the Motel de Ville on Montreal Road. ABOVE, a recent photo shows that the once classic design has been lost.

The mid-century design of the original motel featured a cantilevered roof over the lobby and a very eye-catching sign. This motel later became the Concorde Motel, which is when its unique overhang was chopped off.

The Concorde still exists today, and photos on its website reveal it still has the original bed frames that you can see in 1960s postcards for the Motel de Ville. Props to them for maintaining this unique motel's past. At least on the inside.

The White House

Perhaps copying the capital city to the south of us, Ottawa had its own White House once — a motel at 2583 Carling Avenue. Boasting heated rooms "all year round," this classic motel was located next to Lincoln Fields Shopping Centre, where an all-you-can-eat Chinese Buffet was also once located.

WHITE HOUSE MOTEL
21″ T.V. in every room - Radios
Heated The Year 'Round
One of the Finest Motels in the Ottawa Area
2583 Carling Ave. — Situated on Highway 17 near
Highway 15 and 17 Junction.
OTTAWA, ONTARIO, CANADA.

It seems the White House crumbled and is now just an abandoned building soon to become a self-storage facility. We will keep an eye on the other White House to see if it suffers the same fate as Ottawa's.

The former White House Motel, complete with cool neon sign out front on Carling Avenue. BELOW, the abandoned buffet restaurant that occupies the former White House Motel space, complete with a sign announcing the coming of a Dymon Storage.

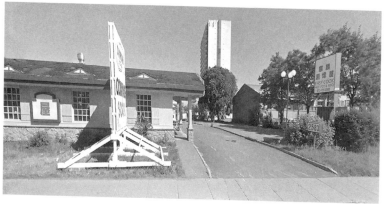

Readers' Remarks

When I go to Flagstaff it is on the old Route 66. There are a lot of little motels like the ones in this story. I wonder how they keep going given the lack of modern amenities. I can't imagine the younger ones holding onto the allure that was their grandparents. — *Mike*

Those were wonderful years. Full employment and prosperity. In those days, the husband's wage not only paid the mortgage, the family car, children's education and the upkeep of the family home ... there was also enough left over for savings which provided family holidays at least once a year. Seeing these photos evokes such happy memories and captures the wonderful atmosphere of those days. — *Robert*

I wound up on your site after finding an old book of matches amongst my father's things. It reads, the "Butler Motor Hotel, Ottawa." Great article, and yes, sad to see that most of these architectural time capsules are gone. — *Jennifer*

The Butler Motor Hotel had an incredible sign out front and equally impressive mid-century architecture. BELOW, the once glorious Butler Motel, now the Ottawa Plaza Inn.

Butler Motor Hotel

Once having a posh butler cartoon character to welcome guests, the Butler Motor Hotel has been so horribly modified from its original form that you may not recognize it as once being "one of the finest motels in Ottawa," complete with a lounge in the basement — the Coachman — which had musical acts in its 1960s heyday. Today, the Ottawa Plaza Inn reveals little of its mid-century past.

Worthy of Preserving

These three motels are but a snapshot of the many motels that once graced Ottawa's streets, a lost form of accommodation for tourists to our city. I often wish Ottawa had followed the lead of California's Palm Springs, by preserving our mid-century modernist motels and commercial architecture.

If we had, we might have attracted tourists and fans not only of our political institutions and beautiful geography, but also the unique commercial architecture we once had.

Macdonald Park is in Lowertown, bordered by Heney, Wurtemberg, Cobourg and Tormey streets. It is just north of Rideau Street, where it meets the Rideau River. It is a tranquil park, enjoyed mostly by locals (it is a hard park to find) who wander its meandering pathways, unaware, likely, that their neighbourhood park was once a cemetery.

Indeed, it was once one of Ottawa's oldest cemeteries, and below the surface of this small park are the forgotten tombstones and skeletal remains of some of our city's earliest residents.

Ottawa's first cemetery was on Elgin Street at the foot of what was Barrack Hill. In 1840, when this plot of land became too small for the growing village, the bodies were moved to what is now Macdonald Park. At the time, this was considered well past the city limits.

This second cemetery opened in 1845 and operated until the 1870s, when again it became too small and had to be relocated. This time the cemetery was moved to Beechwood Avenue, where it remains to this day.

Hundreds of bodies had to be claimed and moved to the new cemetery. Those unlucky enough not to have a family member claim them were left behind. There they remained until 1911, when the City of Ottawa built a new park in honour of Sir John A. Macdonald on the site of the former graveyard.

Also Something About the People Who Resided in That Far North Eastern Corner of Ottawa Fifty Years Ago. District Was Sparsely Settled and Sandy Roads Were Difficult To Negotiate. Tom Alexander Was Quaint Character. Family Lived on Porter's Island.

THIS week we go back fifty years and take a glimpse at the far eastern corner of Sandy Hill—that section bounded on the west by Cobourg, on the east by Wurtemburg, on the south by Rideau and on the north by St. Patrick street. In this endeavor to revive memories of another section of our fair city as it was a full half century ago, we have the valued co-operation of Mr. Hilaire Leger, who has been living in the same house at 26 Cobourg street for forty-nine years, having been among the first few to settle on that street.

To put it in more or less terse language, the few people who inhabited that corner of Sandy Hill a half century ago were those who bore witness to the last anguishing wails of two old cemeteries—two fine old harbingers of the dead which had served their purpose, and over whose sandy loam the ghosts of the past still flitted.

Today at this central point in the area we are concerned with, we gaze upon two picturesque parks—the playground of a new generation. Fifty years ago the last of the claimed bodies had been removed and interred in other burial grounds outside the city and workmen were engaged in the task of levelling off the property preparatory to turning it into a place of beauty—and with the full knowledge that they must proceed with the utmost care lest they disturb the remains of a considerable number of departed citizens who were left in their original repose and who still lie buried under the well kept lawns of Macdonald park.

Just as the park is divided into two sections today, with Charlotte street running through the center of it, so the two old cemeteries were divided in their day; the one on the west was the burial ground for those of the Roman Catholic faith and the one on the east was known as the Anglican cemetery. We are told that when these cemeteries were turned into a park the remaining tombstones were laid flat and covered with earth. Under some of those old tombstones are the remains of pioneer citizens—men and women who walked the streets of Bytown nearly a century and a quarter ago.

An Unearthed Skull.

Mr. Leger tells that one day when he was passing the cemetery which faced on Cobourg street—that part of it which harbored a bathing pool for small children about fifteen years ago—he stopped to watch some workmen cutting down a sandy knoll, and as he stood there he noticed a round object emerge from the top of the knoll and roll into the pit below. His curiosity aroused, he proceeded to investigate and found that it was a human skull, apparently that of a young person, with the teeth still in perfect condition. He picked it up and handed it to one of the workers. What became of it after

On the previous page, an 1885 map shows the circled plot of land labelled as "cemeteries." AT LEFT, a 1936 *Ottawa Citizen* article recounts the time a skull was unearthed in the park. BELOW, the Park of the Dead, or Macdonald Park, surrounded by Ottawa today.

A 1936 *Ottawa Citizen* article tells the story of city workers doing landscaping in the park, only to accidentally unearth the skull of one of the unfortunate souls left behind. It has long been rumoured that the small hill in Macdonald Park, on top of which a stone bandshell has been built, was where the city interred the bodies left behind.

Readers' Remarks

My parents lived on Tormey for 15 years. We loved looking out on and walking through the park. I'm glad to know more of its history. — *Dianne*

I saw a documentary on this years ago. I tried to Google it for a long time. I'm so happy I found it! It's an awesome story! — *Francine*

When the large apartments were planned on Wurtemberg Street, many pieces of coffin hardware were brought up in the large shovel while excavating the deep holes for the building foundation. I worked with Grant Haulage then, in the 1960s and 1970s. — *Jacullen*

I always thought that park looked odd. I have friends living just across the street from it. Now I find out it was a cemetery. Yes, that makes sense. I can see it. — *Larry*

I lived on Tormey Street as a kid and spent a lot of time running up and down that hill. The hill seemed much higher then. Glad I didn't know then what was under "my" park! — *Cathy*

The grounds of Macdonald Park, showing the stone bandshell in the distance. BELOW: An aerial view of the park today..

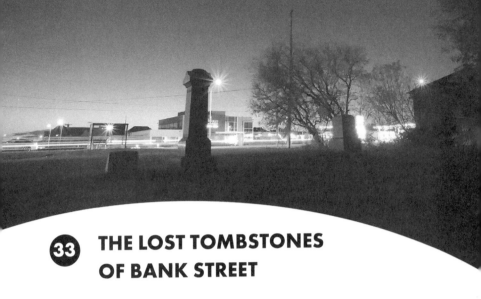

THE LOST TOMBSTONES OF BANK STREET

Bank Street is one of Ottawa's oldest streets. It was there on the first survey of the city drawn by John By, a north-south service road that didn't have a name at first, By being too busy giving lofty names to the roads that mattered — Wellington, Sussex and Elgin.

Only when he saw the service road on his map did it occur to him that it needed a name. He called it Bank, because at that time it started at the banks of the Ottawa River.

Bank Street is also a busy road, taking people into the heart of the city — or out of it — every day. The motorists that drive past Analdea Boulevard on the southern stretch of Bank Street probably take no notice of the three 19th-century tombstones at the busy intersection. Yet, here lies an abandoned graveyard, with those tombstones being the last visible reminder of what was once there.

A Methodist Cemetery

In the 1800s, the grassy plot of land at the corner of Bank and Analdea was a Methodist church and in back of the church, as was customary for the day, there was a cemetery. The intersection is now more or less the gateway to the sprawling suburb of Findlay Creek.

The rural church served the settlement of Gloucester until the 1930s, at which time the congregation was relocated. The church building was purchased in 1940 by the Women's Institute, which used it as a community centre. The community centre then relocated and the church was torn down sometime in the 1970s.

During that nearly 50-year span between the congregation relocating and the church being torn down, most of the bodies in the cemetery out back were reinterred someplace else. But for reasons unknown, not all the graves were moved. Three lonely tombstones remain on Bank Street

One grave is that of baby Herbert, son of May Ann and Robert Goth and aged only four months when he was buried. The baby has inexplicably been separated from the grave of his parents, who lie at another cemetery down the road in Johnston Corners. That cemetery is the final resting place for John Goth, who died in 1897 at the age of 81, and his wife Hannah Goth, who died in 1920 at the age of 96.

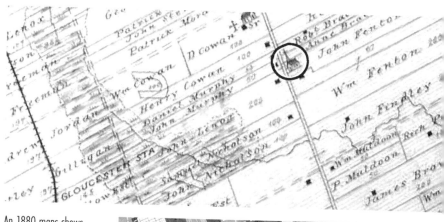

An 1880 maps shows where Gloucester's Methodist Church would have been located.

Aerial view of the intersection of Bank Street and Analdea Drive where the church and cemetery once were.

The lonely graves in an empty lot on Bank Street, near the suburb of Findlay Creek.

Another of the abandoned Bank Street tombstones shows the plot for the Fenton family, with six members of that family buried beneath the marker. Ages of the dead ranged from 23 to 90.

The City of Ottawa maintains the forgotten cemetery as development sprawls in all directions around the lonely graves. They seem out of place on a large tract of prime real estate surrounded by suburban homes.

Perhaps the words on the Goth tombstone reveal the reason why they have been left undisturbed. The tombstone reads: *Not Here Has Risen.*

The final resting place for four-month-old Herbert Goth.

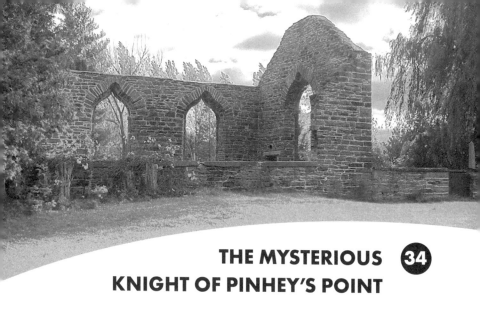

THE MYSTERIOUS 34
KNIGHT OF PINHEY'S POINT

The Knight of Horaceville

Amidst the maples and oaks, almost hidden from view, are the stone ruins of a medieval-style church. It is perched on a high bluff overlooking a picturesque river. You might think you were in Germany or some other European country — but you're just twenty minutes upriver from Ottawa.

The ruins are part of Horaceville, a settlement that was never a settlement in the traditional sense. It was part of a palatial estate built by Hamnett Kirkes Pinhey, an Englishman who arrived in 1820 after receiving a land grant for his service during the Napoleonic Wars.

Traveling by boat up the Ottawa River, Pinhey picked a hillside location with a sheltered bay about twenty kilometres north of what was soon to become Bytown as the place to create his utopian vision of a gentleman's estate. Pinhey built a small log cabin to live in for his first winter in Upper Canada, and his family joined him the next summer.

The Pinheys were going to need more than a log cabin. The family arrived with 55 steamer crates of furnishings, books, clothing and dinnerware. Pinhey happily went about building his village (named after his son) along with his stately manor home, mills, barns and, eventually, the church.

↑ The ruins of St. Mary's Church, built by Hamnett Pinhey in the 1820s.

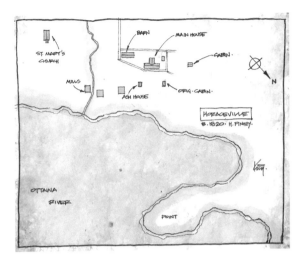

Establishing himself as a man of prominence, he entered politics as a member of the pre-Confederation Province of Canada's Legislative Assembly. Pinhey died in 1857 but left behind an interesting legacy and an intriguing question — was this gentleman squire a secret knight?

Knights Hospitaller

The Knights Hospitaller are a medieval order of knights with connections to the better-known Knights Templar. The Order still exists today as the Knights of Saint John. You may recognize the name and their symbol, the Maltese Cross, as the St. John Ambulance logo.

St. John Ambulance follows the structure of the original Order of Knights Hospitaller and is divided internationally into priories, which reflects the history of the original Order.

The Knights Hospitallers and the Knights Templars trained and

Knights of the orders of Templar (left) and Hospitaller (right) wearing their respective armour. Note the Maltese Cross on the tunic of the Hospitallier and on the emblem of St. John Ambulance logo.

fought together, protecting and caring for pilgrims to the Holy Land during the Crusades. Originally the Order was only of a "hospital" nature, but it soon provided pilgrims with an armed escort, which grew into an imposing force with both the Hospitallers and Templars becoming formidable military orders in the Holy Land.

After the disestablishment of both the Templars and Hospitallers, it wasn't until 1831 that a British order of these knights was founded again. They became known as the "Most Venerable Order of St. John of Jerusalem."

In Pinhey's original cabin there are some decaying logs and a stone fireplace with unusual symbols carved into the stonework. Two equilateral triangular symbols with intersecting lines are marked within the fireplace, perhaps modern mason marks from a recent restoration, yet they prompted me to take a closer look at what I felt was an unusual aesthetic to the property.

Pinhey's main house is an asymmetric design of oddly placed windows and louvered fake doors, which could likely be attributed to it being built in multiple stages as his wealth slowly transferred from England to his estate in Canada. However, an aerial view of the main house reveals the house has a very symmetrical T-shape.

Whether by coincidence or by Georgian architecture standards,

Pinhey's original log cabin and the symbol that is carved into its fireplace — a symbol that is identical in shape and proportions to the house he designed.

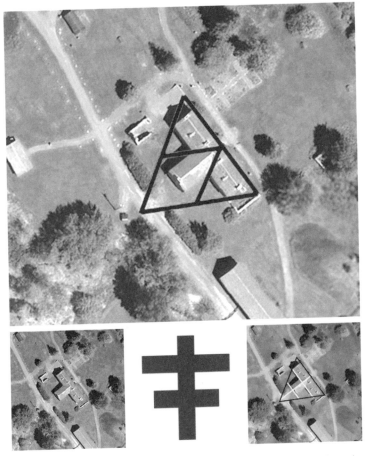

These photos show the Cross of the Grand Priory (bottom centre) and the Order of the Holy Royal Arch, when superimposed over an aerial photo of Pinhey's manor-estate building.

this t-shaped footprint of the house fits perfectly within an equilateral triangle, the same triangle that is carved into the original cabin fireplace. The house shape is also of such proportions that once placed inside an equilateral triangle, dissecting the lines within it reveals other shapes that coincide with recognizable shapes from Freemasonry.

The symbols of the Cross of the Grand Priory, the Order of the Holy Royal Arch and, even more relevant, the Maltese Cross of the Knights Hospitaller are all visible when superimposed on the house's shape.

Holy of Holies

On the second floor of the estate, there is a room that is known as the Sanctum Sanctorum, which is Latin for Holy of Holies. The Holy of Holies is among the most sacred site in Judaism, an inner sanctuary within the Temple in Jerusalem, when Solomon's Temple was still standing. The Holy of Holies was located in the westernmost end of the temple building, being a perfect cube: 20 cubits by 20 cubits by 20 cubits.

The inside was in total darkness and allegedly contained the Ark of the Covenant, gilded inside and out, in which was placed the Tablets of the Covenant. It is also where the Knights Templar made their headquarters in a wing of the royal palace on the Temple Mount in the captured Al-Aqsa Mosque.

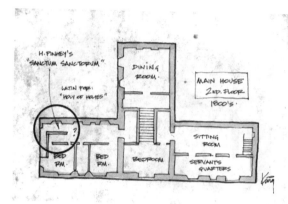

Plan of the second floor of the main house showing the location of the sanctum sanctoriam in the west wing.

The Temple Mount had a mystique because it was above what was believed to be the ruins of the Temple of Solomon, leading to the knights' name of "Templar" knights. Pinhey's Holy of Holies has not been measured, but it would be interesting to see if he made it in the same dimensions.

Pinhey's Church

Doing further research into Pinhey and this marvelous estate, I discovered Pinhey constructed his own building of worship on the property against the wishes of the local parish that wanted a church built further inland. Pinhey used his own money to build a church of his own design, constructing it in a style unlike any other church of the area. This church, now part of the Anglican Parish of March, lies in ruins, hidden from view on private property.

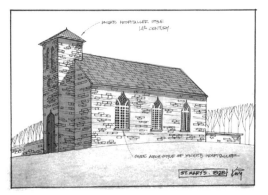

LEFT: A sketch of the stone church built by Pinhey in 1827. Its unique style of architecture resembles that of a medieval English church of the Knights Templar, shown below, with the "ogee" arch windows and doors and a prominent square tower with pyramid roof. RIGHT: The front door of St. Mary's Church with the ogee arch. BELOW: These special and complex arches used by the Hospitallers reflect a Middle Eastern influence from the times they occupied the Holy Land.

Built by Pinhey in 1827, the stone church displays a unique style of architecture that resembles medieval English churches. Pinhey designed it based on sketches from his notebook. Symmetrically constructed with "ogee" arch windows and doors and a prominent square tower with a pyramid roof, it is quite similar to Knights Hospitaller churches.

Similar design elements in both Hospitaller churches and Pinhey's church include the pyramid roofed square tower and these Middle Eastern "ogee" arches. Perhaps it is pure coincidence but it seems odd that Pinhey would utilize the expensive ogee stone arch forms in a church being built at his own expense.

The Final Clues

Upon his death in 1857, Pinhey was buried in a "box tomb" on the west end of the church. The church fell into ruins at the turn of the 20th century, although it remains the oldest standing church within the City of Ottawa. It has been given Heritage Designation as outlined by the Ontario Heritage Act but is not part of the City Of Ottawa's Pinhey's Point Historic Site and remains inaccessible to the general public.

There is no official mention of Pinhey's connection to the Knights Hospitallers at the site, although clues abound throughout the property.

All these clues seem to lead to the conclusion that Pinhey was, or was trying to be, part of an ancient Order of Knights.

I still wasn't satisfied, though, so I dug further and found an 1857 book at the New York Public Library entitled *Synoptical Sketch of the Illustrious & Sovereign Order of Knights Hospitallers of St. John of Jerusalem, and the Venerable Langue of England* which comprehensively lists all members of the Order of Knights from its inception in 1099 to 1857.

On page 75 there is this listing: *The Honourable Hamnett Pinhey, of Horaceville, Canada, Member of the Canadian Legislature, and one of the Governors of Christ's Hospital, London.*

Upon his death in 1857, Pinhey was buried in a "box tomb" on the west end of the church. His tomb is similar to Knights Hospitaller tombs.

35 A NAZI-FIGHTING SNOWMOBILE

Ottawa has been home to a number of secret projects over the years, from the Ottawa Project (see page 50) to the world's first UFO monitoring station. At the height of World War II, the newly formed National Research Council ran a raft of secret projects, some of which we may never hear about.

Some of those once-classified programs included the development of atomic energy, radar technology and the lesser-known development of a classified top secret "snow vehicle" designed to shut down the German nuclear program.

The Allies knew Germany was doing atomic weapons research in Rjukan, Norway, and in March 1942 an eccentric British inventor by the name of Geoffrey Pyke proposed an idea to Lord Louis Mountbatten, Chief of Combined Operations Headquarters in England. Pyke's idea was to have allied commandoes parachute into Norway and establish a base for commando attacks against the German army stationed there to protect the research facility.

Pyke wanted the commandoes equipped with a snow vehicle light enough to be parachuted in with them, yet durable and powerful enough to makes its way through all types of snow. The British realized they did not have the industry or knowledge to design such a vehicle and asked the U.S. for help. The U.S. in turn called upon another ally with more experience with snow and cold: Canada.

The National Research Council in Ottawa was given the project. Working at the NRC at the time was scientist George Klein, who was doing research on the interaction of snow and ice with other materials. He was put in charge of developing the vehicle, which was soon given the codename WEASEL.

(Klein would go on to have an illustrious career at the NRC, helping to develop the CanadArm for NASA's Space Shuttle, the electric wheelchair and the CANDU nuclear reactor.)

TOP: The Chateau Laurier where George Klein and Geoffrey Pyke drew up plans for the classified snow vehicle. TOP RIGHT: George Klein, the scientist who developed the WEASEL. BELOW: The National Research Council on Sussex Drive, where secret World War II projects were developed.

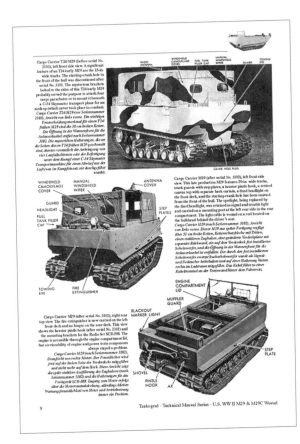

The Ottawa-designed WEASEL, a heavily fortified snowmobile, as produced by Studebaker during World War II.

Made for the Devil's Brigade

In June of 1942, Pyke came to Ottawa from England and he and Klein pored over design ideas at the Chateau Laurier. Klein got to work immediately and the vehicle began development at the NRC labs on Sussex Drive.

At the same time, the Americans started training the commandoes that would man the vehicles. It would be a joint taskforce of Americans and Canadians, a special-forces unit that would become famous later by its unofficial name, The Devil's Brigade.

With the training underway in Montana, Klein's team had less than 12 months to develop a prototype of the snow vehicle. He met the deadline and the U.S. military contracted the Studebaker Corporation to manufacture the vehicle. Studebaker used a Model 6-170

The WEASEL in action during World War II.

Champion engine, a six-cylinder 169.6 cu. in. (2,779 cc) four-stroke engine delivering 70 bhp at 3,600 rpm.

Klein's Ottawa design called for full tracks of rubber instead of the usual half-tracks with skis. The Studebaker engineers didn't like the design and went with an all-metal track. After the prototype WEASELS underwent tests in Alberta, the metal tracks and components iced up and it was realized that Klein's original design was better.

Studebaker manufactured 15,000 WEASELS with the full-rubber tracks but the commando raid on Norway was cancelled and the unique vehicle was used instead on the beaches of Normandy, the swamps of the Pacific Theatre, and after the war, in both Arctic and Antarctic exploration.

36 THE OTTAWA X-FILES

At an intersection in east-end Ottawa you will find Scully Way and Mulder Road, streets named after the lead characters in the hit sci-fi TV series, *The X-Files*.

The streets were named by Claridge Homes. According to news reports from 2001, the company was given a list of approved street names by the municipality of Cumberland, and Scully was on the list. A company spokesperson told the *Ottawa Citizen*, "Well, [Scully] had been approved. Mulder seemed the obvious choice for a street to intersect with it."

A fun suburban tribute to television sci-fi. But is it a tribute? What if Ottawa is the perfect city for a Scully-Mulder intersection? Check out these stories from Ottawa's very own X-Files.

Jam Band

In November 2005, hundreds of Ottawa residents were affected by a mysterious signal that jammed their automatic garage door openers. The phenomenon occurred within a 25-mile radius, and included

embassy gates and residential homes between Aylmer and Casselman.

Almost all automatic garage door openers operate with a remote that uses a radio signal on the 390 MHZ band, but on that day the remotes were rendered inoperable. Further investigation showed the 390 MHZ signal is also employed by Land Mobile Radio Systems, which is used by the United States government, and a December 2005 U.S. Government Accountability Office report coincidentally states:

> This might explain Ottawa's curious locked-garage-door incident, except both the Canadian military and the U.S. Embassy categorically denied using this new technology. Industry Canada inspectors arrived in Ottawa to study the signal jamming but as they began to investigate the problem it disappeared and all systems returned to normal.

No explanation has ever been given for what happened in the autumn of 2005. The garage doors remained closed for ten days.

An Underwater UFO

In July 2009, a number of military helicopters were circling the Ottawa River by the Champlain Bridge and in typical Spielbergian fashion, I grabbed my bike and hastily pedalled my way down to the river to  see what all the commotion was about. Search and rescue helicopters, military vehicles and several Ottawa Police vehicles had gathered around the river in what looked like a complex recovery operation.

Further investigation revealed that the previous night people in Ottawa and in Gatineau had reported seeing an object streak across the night sky and crash into the Ottawa River with a thunderous boom. The object reportedly had lights on and appeared to change course several times before it hit the water.

Because there were multiple reports, police, firefighters, paramedics and a helicopter from CFB Trenton scoured the waters the next day searching for a downed aircraft. Using sonar and underwater cameras the search team soon found an object about 30 feet below the surface. An article quoted police constable Alain Boucher saying of the object, "The size and the shape don't lead us to believe it's any piece of an airplane or fuselage or anything like that. It could be a rock, it could be a bunch of logs stuck together, it's hard to say."

The next day police told media that because no aircraft had been reported missing, and because there was no debris or oil slick on the river, the search was being terminated. No further investigation was done into what happened on the river that July night, and the incident remains a mystery.

The Barrhaven Beast

In 2015 a "mystery creature" viciously attacked a horse in the NCC's Greenbelt, near the suburban community of Barrhaven. NCC officials

described the attack as a "wildlife incident" and closed off trails in the area. Conservation officers then lay traps in the forest in an effort to capture whatever attacked the horse.

The owner of the horse told media that it was "no coyote" and the *Ottawa Sun* reported that Dr. Brent Patterson, a wildlife expert with the Ontario Ministry of Natural Resources, had studied the photos of the horse's wounds and ruled out coyotes, bobcats or cougars as possible culprits.

So what attacked the horse? A nearby farmer reported a cougar was spotted in his barn, but that animal had been ruled out as the attacker. The traps never caught anything and the area was soon reopened. Speculation ranged from a bear, rabid dog, a fisher or possibly even the legendary "chupacabra," an odd beast rumoured to inhabit parts of the Americas.

The name comes from the animal's reported habit of attacking and drinking the blood of livestock. A chupacabra is described as a heavy creature, the size of a small bear, with a row of spines reaching from the neck to the base of the tail. Eyewitness sightings have been reported as far north as Maine. Most wildlife experts say the chupacabra is probably a coyote infected with a parasite. The perplexing case of the Barrhaven Beast remains unsolved.

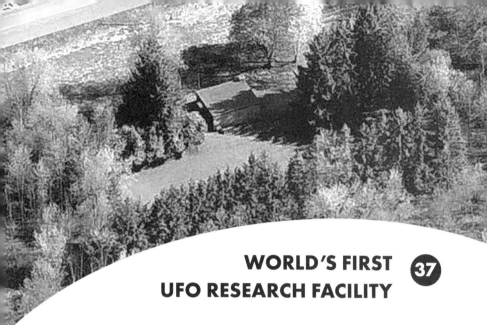

WORLD'S FIRST UFO RESEARCH FACILITY

During the 1950s there seemed to be almost weekly reports in the media of Unidentified Flying Objects (UFOs.) How governments around the world responded to these reports is the source of much conjecture to this day.

What is not conjecture is that the Canadian government took the reports seriously enough to establish the world's first UFO research facility.

Established by the Canadian Department of Transport (DOT), the Unidentified Flying Object Research Program was put under the direction of Wilbert B. Smith, senior radio engineer for the DOT's Broadcast and Measurements Section. Smith, working with the Defence Research Board and the National Research Council, set out to determine not only if UFOs existed, but if they might hold the key to a new source of power, perhaps using the sun's magnetic field as a form of propulsion.

Smith's geo-magnetic studies grew, and in 1952 the investigation was moved to Shirley's Bay and a government facility on the Ottawa River. UFO detection equipment was installed and by the end of October of 1952 the installation was complete. It became the world's first UFO research facility.

Aerial view of the UFO research facility at Shirley's Bay before its 2011 demolition.

Wilbert B. Smith

The 12-foot by 12-foot building housed instruments such as a gamma-ray counter, a magnetometer, a radio receiver (to detect the presence of radio noise) and a recording gravimeter with a 50-mile radius from the station.

Smith and his UFO research tried to attract UFOs to the area using their newly installed equipment. After months of recording potential UFO activity in the area, the facility soon had its most unusual occurrence.

Calling any UFO

At 3:01 p.m. on August 8, 1954, the instrumentation at the Shirley's Bay facility registered an unusual disturbance. In Smith's words, "the gravimeter went wild." The gravimeter reading meant a greater deflection was registered than could be explained by conventional interference, such as a passing aircraft. Smith and his colleagues rushed outside to see what was creating such an enormous reading on their equipment.

Once outside the research building they were disappointed to find a heavily overcast sky with limited visibility. Whatever kind of craft was up there was well hidden. The only evidence the researchers had of an unusual flying object in the area that day was the deflection registered on the chart-recorder paper.

Two days after the incident the Shirley's Bay research facility was abruptly shut down upon orders from the Department of Transport. Many speculate the findings and strange occurrence at Shirley's Bay prompted the project to go "underground," with any new findings to be classified as top secret.

A conspiracy theory, perhaps, but there were indeed some oddities about the closure of the Shirley's Bay facility, including the fact it never actually closed. While funding for the UFO research facility was terminated, Smith continued working at Shirley's Bay.

A few years later he claimed to have developed a revolutionary anti-gravity device. In a 1959 presentation, Smith stated, "We have

LEFT: UFO Monitoring equipment installed at Shirley's Bay in 1952. RIGHT: Monitoring the equipment.

conducted experiments that show that it is possible to create artificial gravity (not centrifugal force) and to alter the gravitational field of the Earth. This we have done. It is fact. The next step is to learn the rules and do the engineering necessary to convert the principle into workable hardware."

Building 67

As Smith was about to finish work on this anti-gravity device he was stricken with cancer and died at the age of 52 on December 27, 1962. The research facility at Shirley's Bay was finally closed. The building he worked in became part of the Shirley's Bay Department of National Defence complex, now known as the Defence Research and Development Canada complex, off Carling Avenue.

Smith's workplace was marked as Building 67 on maps of the complex, but it was torn down in 2011. The exact nature of his research, and what happened in the skies over Ottawa on August 8, 1954, may never be known. Although, perhaps, the truth is out there.

Machine 'Records' Saucer'

OTTAWA — (CP) — Is Canada the first country in the world to record a flying saucer with instruments?

That question is being debated here today after the transport department's flying saucer sighting station reported that it had detected an unexplained object in the atmosphere over Ottawa Sunday.

Wilbert B. Smith, engineer in charge of the broadcast and measurement section of the transport department, said the saucer station's gravimeter was tripped at 3:01 p.m.

The gravimeter is designed to detect and record gamma rays, magnetic fluctuations, radio noises and gravity and mass changes in the atmosphere.

38 WHAT'S WITH THAT BRIDGE?

A Smiths Falls landmark for over a century, the giant iron bridge on the outskirts of town that once spanned the Rideau Canal sits like a massive sentinel, forever poised at a 45-degree angle.

Built by the Canadian Northern Railway between 1912-13, the bridge was part of the Toronto-to-Ottawa connection of the CNR. Designed in Chicago and built by the Dominion Bridge Company, this massive iron bridge showcased a new style of bridge engineering that was fairly new to North America.

Called the Scherzer Rolling Lift Bascule Bridge, after the Chicago company that designed it, these bridges were intended for areas where a high rail bridge or swing bridge could not be implemented. Bascule is French for "see-saw," the principle used in its design and operation.

Using a perfectly balanced concrete counterweight, the bridge lifted up with relative ease by either manual or electric operation. The bridge first began operating by manual fashion, but in 1914 a DC electric motor was installed. In 1915, the town of Smiths Falls switched to AC electric current, making the bridge motor useless. It went back to being manually operated.